Reclaiming Wonder

Incitements

Series editors
Peg Birmingham, DePaul University
and Dimitris Vardoulakis, Western Sydney University

Editorial Advisory Board
Étienne Balibar, Andrew Benjamin, Jay M. Bernstein, Rosi Braidotti, Wendy Brown, Judith Butler, Adriana Cavarero, Howard Caygill, Rebecca Comay, Joan Copjec, Simon Critchley, Costas Douzinas, Peter Fenves, Christopher Fynsk, Moira Gatens, Gregg Lambert, Leonard Lawlor, Genevieve Lloyd, Catherine Malabou, James Martel, Christoph Menke, Warren Montag, Michael Naas, Antonio Negri, Kelly Oliver, Paul Patton, Anson Rabinbach, Gerhard Richter, Martin Saar, Miguel Vatter, Gianni Vattimo, Santiago Zabala

Available

Return Statements: The Return of Religion in Contemporary Philosophy
Gregg Lambert

The Refusal of Politics
Laurent Dubreuil, translated by Cory Browning

Plastic Sovereignties: Agamben and the Politics of Aesthetics
Arne De Boever

*From Violence to Speaking Out:
Apocalypse and Expression in Foucault, Derrida and Deleuze*
Leonard Lawlor

Agonistic Mourning: Political Dissidence and the Women in Black
Athena Athanasiou

Interpassivity: The Aesthetics of Delegated Enjoyment
Robert Pfaller

Derrida's Secret: Perjury, Testimony, Oath
Charles Barbour

Resistance and Psychoanalysis: Impossible Divisions
Simon Morgan Wortham

Visit the series web page at: edinburghuniversitypress.com/series/incite

Reclaiming Wonder

After the Sublime

Genevieve Lloyd

EDINBURGH
University Press

Edinburgh University Press is one of the leading university presses in the UK. We publish academic books and journals in our selected subject areas across the humanities and social sciences, combining cutting-edge scholarship with high editorial and production values to produce academic works of lasting importance. For more information visit our website: edinburghuniversitypress.com

© Genevieve Lloyd, 2018

Edinburgh University Press Ltd
The Tun – Holyrood Road, 12(2f) Jackson's Entry, Edinburgh EH8 8PJ

Typeset in Bembo
by R. J. Footring Ltd, Derby, UK

A CIP record for this book is available from the British Library

ISBN 978 1 4744 3310 5 (hardback)
ISBN 978 1 4744 3312 9 (webready PDF)
ISBN 978 1 4744 3311 2 (paperback)
ISBN 978 1 4744 3313 6 (epub)

The right of Genevieve Lloyd to be identified as the author of this work has been asserted in accordance with the Copyright, Designs and Patents Act 1988, and the Copyright and Related Rights Regulations 2003 (SI No. 2498).

Contents

Acknowledgements vii

Introduction 1
[1] Pause for Thought: Plato and Aristotle on Wonder 15
[2] Passion or Distraction? Descartes and Spinoza on Wonder 30
[3] Burke and Kant on the Sublime 52
[4] Romanticism and the Allure of the Sublime 73
[5] Wonder and Stupidity: Flaubert on Romanticism 92
[6] Reconnecting with Socratic Wonder: Heidegger and Arendt 120
[7] Derrida on *Aporia*, Time and Mortality 140
[8] Political Wonder and Social Critique 155
[9] Wonder and Transcendence 183
Conclusion: The Future of Wonder 205

Bibliography 221
Index 228

Acknowledgements

An earlier version of material from Chapters 1, 2 and 7 was delivered in a lecture to the Australian Society for Continental Philosophy Annual Conference, held at the Melbourne Campus of the Australian Catholic University, 4-6 December 2014, and subsequently published under the title 'Derrida and the Philosophical History of Wonder', in *Parrhesia: A Critical Journal of Philosophy*, No. 24, 2015, pp. 64-82. Related material also occurs in passages included in my essay, 'The Philosophical History of Wonder', published in *Graduate Faculty Philosophy Journal*, The New School for Social Research, Vol. 34, No. 2, 2013, pp. 299-316. Some passages in my discussion, in Chapter 8, of Arendt's comments on asylum seekers occur also, differently framed, in my essay, 'Nomadic Subjects and Asylum Seekers', in Bolette Blaagaard and Iris Van Der Tuin, eds, *The Subject of Rosi Braidotti: Politics and Concepts* (London: Bloomsbury, 2014), pp. 185-9.

I am grateful to Amélie Rorty for her interest in earlier versions of the material, and to Edinburgh University Press readers for helpful responses during preparation of the final version. I wish also to express my appreciation to the series editors, Peg Birmingham and Dimitris Vardoulakis, for encouraging the

ACKNOWLEDGEMENTS

project, and to all involved in the production process: to Carol Macdonald, Ersev Ersoy and James Dale for professional advice and thoughtful suggestions, and to Tim Clark for meticulous and constructive copy editing.

Introduction

Philosophers once delighted in wonder, to the point where they claimed it as their own – as a special state of mind which defined their distinctive intellectual activity. Today's philosophers, in contrast, show few signs of thinking about wonder at all. Wonder is curiously absent from contemporary philosophical concerns. It has, it seems, been relegated to the past. Philosophers still happily acknowledge that it may – as their ancient counterparts thought – have been the beginnings of their mode of thinking; it may have stimulated the emergence of philosophy from misty myth into the clearer light of intellectual inquiry. However, contemporary philosophy seems more eager to identify with the rigorous methodical processes associated with modern science than with the stirrings of wonder.

Something of that old narrative of philosophy's progress – from myth and metaphor into the clear light of reason – seems to be mirrored in more general attitudes to wonder. Wonder tends to be appreciated, even cherished, in its manifestations in the very young. The capacity for wonder is commonly seen as an endearing trait of childhood; its charms are less beguiling in adulthood. We may regret the decline of that capacity – along with other inevitable costs of the benefits of maturity. Having put aside childish things, we are in our adult lives uncertain what to think about wonder — and about how to think with it. If we browse in bookshops for expressions of wonder, we are more likely to find them under 'Fantasy Fiction' than in the Philosophy sections. Non-recreational wonder — along with sustained philosophical consideration of its nature and of its role in the life of the mind — seems to have gone missing. Wonder is now generally associated with escapist retreat into the fantastic, rather than with serious intellectual engagement with reality.

Our collective uncertainty about wonder is not surprising. Ambivalence about it has pervaded the history of western thought, becoming more acute with the development of modern science. Even in those distant times when philosophers were happy to define themselves through it, wonder was associated with intellectual discontent. Indeed, discontent was often seen as inherent in it. To be prone to wonder indicated a lack of knowledge; and it was the sense of that lack, after all, that made wonder the driving force of inquiry.

Wonder can have negative associations — as restless fluctuation. It can also have positive associations — as purposeful desire. It can be construed as a balancing or reconciliation between opposed tendencies to motion and rest. All these attitudes to wonder can be found in the history of western philosophy. The history of wonder is not the simple trajectory of a single concept. It reflects a variety of ways of thinking about knowledge. It has been intermingled with the history of other emotions such as awe and dread; it has also been caught up in changing attitudes towards imagination. It has been associated with surprise and amazement, and hence sometimes with stupor. By extension, it has been related to stupidity, as well as to intense intelligence and intellectual activity. Through its connotations of transcendence, mystery and awe, it has been caught up in the history of religion; it has been a focal point, especially, for contention about modern ideas of the secular.

Wonder's role in the acquisition of knowledge is only one thread in its long history; yet that thread has at times dominated the tapestry. Wonder's other aspects can be difficult to extricate from familiar narratives of its role in instigating inquiry, and of its limitations as a source of new knowledge. Yet wonder can be directed to things we already know, as well as to what remains unknown. We can wonder at everyday things, as well as being amazed by the strange and exotic. Wonder can also have political significance; it can shake us into a fresh perception of what is at stake in cultural assumptions and expectations that we have come to regard as normal.

This book is an attempt to reconnect with the philosophical past of wonder, and to defend its continuing importance in the life of the mind. Beginning from Plato's treatment of it in his Socratic Dialogues, and Aristotle's in the *Metaphysics*, it traces a succession of ways in which past philosophers have conceptualised wonder through the idea of a hiatus in mental activity. Frequently, that association with interrupted mental activity has given rise to a suspicion of wonder's influence. The implied pause in thought has been seen as a source of debilitating passivity, at odds with the effort to understand. However, it has also been seen in a more positive light – as connecting wonder with purposeful desire and contributing to a sense of intellectual pleasure and well-being.

The Platonic strand in the history of wonder connects it with the search for wisdom; the Aristotelian strand focuses more on its role in the right methods for theoretical inquiry. Those strands are not always in conflict, nor can their historical trajectories be readily separated. However, in the seventeenth century, the tensions between them surfaced in a sharp division between the accounts of wonder offered by Descartes and by Spinoza.

Chapter 1, 'Pause for Thought', discusses the ancient Greek treatments of wonder. It focuses on Plato's treatment of its relations to philosophical inquiry in the *Theaetetus*, and his idea – developed in other Dialogues – of the philosopher as the critical 'gadfly' of society. It also engages with the emphasis that Aristotelian philosophy gave to wonder's connections with desire and pleasure. Plato highlighted wonder's connections with coming to know. Aristotle, in contrast, stressed the end-state of the process – the mind's coming to rest in knowledge. The difference was one of emphasis, rather than a conflict between rival accounts of the nature of wonder. Each gave priority to consideration of a different stage in a single process of thought. Aristotle's praise of the end-state as 'more noble' than the beginning was, nonetheless, an early intimation of a privileging of certainty over 'not-knowing' that would recur throughout the philosophical history of wonder.

Chapter 2, 'Passion or Distraction?', moves on to the seventeenth century to explore the issues at stake in Spinoza's vehement repudiation of Descartes' treatment of wonder. Both philosophers saw wonder as involving a hiatus in mental activity. However, while Descartes, in his *Passions of the Soul*, gave wonder the status of a 'primary passion', Spinoza, in his *Ethics*, did not allow it the status of a passion at all. It was a difference which was to prove significant in later developments.

Although he praised the role of wonder in knowledge, Descartes warned that it should be treated with caution: having stimulated the mind to begin inquiry, it can come to impede that intellectual activity. For Spinoza, in contrast, wonder coexists with and strengthens the pursuit of knowledge, rather than impeding it; and it has connections with other aspects of mental activity which make it an important intellectual resource. His treatment of wonder's relations with imagination – and, through that, of its centrality in the collective life of the mind – was highly significant in the later philosophical history of wonder.

Spinoza developed those insights in his political writings, criticising the ways in which biblical stories of wonders and miracles had been exploited to inhibit the acceptance of scientific procedures of inquiry. Such narratives, he argued, were social fictions – with a role different from that of scientific explanation. It was an insight which brought the consideration of wonder to bear on the operations of power in social groups.

Those broader aspects of Spinoza's treatment of the inter-relations between imagination and emotion also made his approach to wonder an important precondition for the emergence of notions of 'the sublime' which – as elaborated by Edmund Burke and Immanuel Kant – came, through German Idealism, to shape Romantic sensibility. The concept of the sublime had, in its own right, a significant influence in art, literature and aesthetic theory. Less commonly appreciated has been its role in the transformation of older ways of thinking of wonder.

The idea of the sublime entered eighteenth-century philosophy largely through the circulation in translation of an ancient text, *On the Sublime*, attributed to Longinus. Under its influence – especially through Burke's early work, *A Philosophical Enquiry into the Sublime and Beautiful* – the understanding of wonder came to be split between two conditions. On the one hand, there was *curiosity*, associated with the pursuit of inquiry; on the other hand, there was a more intense and overwhelming state associated with astonishment, awe and dread.

One of the most significant aspects of that split was that, on Burke's account, the powerful effects of the sublime on human minds operated largely independently of reason. Clearly, the feeling of the sublime had continuities with older ideas of wonder. However, the earlier accounts had evoked wonder's profound intellectual depths. In the idea of the sublime, the emphasis was rather on a sense of horrified delight at things apparently beyond the reach of reason. Later, Kant would reclaim the sublime for reason; but he did so in ways that had far-reaching consequences for the understanding of wonder. The Kantian sublime replaced wonder as the feeling most closely related to the mind's capacity for reason. Reason itself, indeed, became the only appropriate object of this intense version of wonder.

Chapter 3, on Burke and Kant, tells the story of the implications for wonder of eighteenth-century theories of the sublime. Among the most important parts of the story is the way Kant's treatment of the sublime relocates the experience of wonder. Rather than being a specific emotion, presented as an object to the Understanding, the Kantian sublime is a product of a dynamic interplay between the rival faculties of the human mind – Imagination, Understanding and Reason. My discussion here draws on a reading offered by Gilles Deleuze, which highlights the power and intensity of the struggle between Reason and Imagination in what was, for Kant, a unified project across his three *Critiques*. Deleuze argues that this emphasis on the stretching of the limits of each faculty, and on the conflicts that arise between them, makes the treatment of the sublime in Kant's *Critique of Judgement* a crucial influence on Romanticism.

The Kantian treatment of the sublime was absorbed into developments in Romantic thought – along with some elements of Spinoza's philosophy. There are conceptual changes involved in those appropriations and adaptations, some of which are addressed in Chapter 4, 'Romanticism and the Allure of the Sublime'. German Idealism drew on Spinoza's key doctrines of mind and matter as attributes of the one Substance, and of the essence of the human mind as consisting in a striving for understanding. Those ideas, however, did not always pass into Romanticism in ways that were true to their sources. Nor did the appropriation of the Kantian sublime always acknowledge the nuances of his treatment of the relations between Reason and Imagination.

Just as important for understanding what became of wonder in Romanticism are the changes in mood and tone that accompanied those conceptual shifts. The emotional intensity of the sublime lingered in Romanticism, and continued to inspire art and literature after the Kantian exultation in the power of Reason had waned. Chapter 4 addresses the continuing allure of the sublime through a reading of Mary Shelley's popular Gothic tale, *Frankenstein*, as a literary exploration of the idea of the sublime in popular consciousness. The sublime is a constant presence throughout the work: in its rendering of the exalted excitement surrounding the quest for discovery – whether in voyages of exploration or in relation to scientific inquiry; in the descriptions of landscape; in the horror elicited by the appearance of the creature resulting from Frankenstein's experimentation; or in the pervasive intermingling of exhilaration and dread.

The chapter concludes with a brief discussion of a retrospective assessment of the allure of the sublime offered by Sylviane Agacinski, in a reading of Kierkegaard's *Fear and Trembling*. She argues that the sublime – with its attendant mood of unsatisfiable yearning for the infinite – can no longer be appropriated into a contemporary consciousness shaped by the acknowledgement of finitude.

Chapter 5 continues the story of the sublime in the thought and sensibility of Romanticism, tracing its demise – from Romantic Idealism to the ambivalent anti-Romanticism of Gustave Flaubert's novels and his reflections on art and literature. It discusses some scenes from *Madame Bovary* as illustrative of the tensions in Flaubert's attitude to ideas of the sublime, before moving on to consider more directly his views on the interconnections between wonder and stupidity.

To draw connections between wonder and stupidity may seem far-fetched. Yet its associations with states of *stupor* or *stupefaction* are not just accidents of terminology. Wonder and stupidity can seem very different states. Yet their paths have crossed throughout the history of philosophy, and that history has left its residue in modern attitudes to knowledge. Flaubert shows that wonder and stupidity belong together; that they coexist and interact. There are some striking commonalities here with older philosophical ideas of wonder: the imagery of motion and rest; the intermingling of intellect and emotion. His theoretical reflections explore the possibility of a state which hovers between not-knowing and knowing – a condition not unlike that in the old accounts of wonder.

Flaubert does not offer rigorous theoretical accounts of the nature of either wonder or stupidity. Yet his works give striking literary expression to their interrelations. It was in his final novel, the unfinished dark comedy *Bouvard and Pecuchet*, and the *Dictionary of Received Ideas* – an assemblage of often repeated inanities, which was intended to accompany it – that Flaubert engaged most directly with what he saw as operations of collective stupidity. Through his characters' frantic search for knowledge he offers a trenchant satire on what he sees as the mentality of his times: the collectively self-imposed curtailing of human possibilities through a failure of imagination. What emerges is that distrust of wonder can give rise to a habitual privileging of established 'conclusions' over active thinking or deliberative judgement. The piteous fate Flaubert gives to Bouvard and Pecuchet enacts the separation of wonder from the pursuit of knowledge.

Chapter 6, 'Reconnecting with Socratic Wonder', engages with twentieth-century attempts to reconnect with Plato's vision of wonder. Under the influence of ideas of the sublime on popular imagination, wonder's older associations with intellectual inquiry and knowledge receded. Much of the magnetism of Plato's dramatisation of Socratic questioning had already weakened under the impact of the rigorous, systematic methods of modern empirical science. Those procedures focused on the appeal of the end-state of objective certainty, rather than on the excitement of the uncertain process of getting there. The wonder that Plato had Socrates describe as 'beginning' philosophy was an intense, 'giddying' state. The calmer state of 'curiosity' which replaced it was more readily eclipsed. The excitement traditionally associated with wonder shifted to the surviving fragments of the Romantic sublime.

The mental unrest induced by the not-yet-known is not always the mere passing pangs of unsatisfied curiosity. Not all wonder is allayed by explanation. Wonder that things are as they are can persist – even when inquiry into what they are, and how they came to be that way, has come to its natural end. The most significant modern voice articulating a sense of loss with regard to the common understanding of wonder is that of Martin Heidegger. He talked in *Being and Time* of a contemplative form of thought that 'wonders at Being'. In related published lectures, he developed the idea of a kind of wonder that is directed at the strangeness of the everyday – a disturbing force of the mysterious within the ordinary. Heidegger finds in this notion the possibility of a modern restatement of the old Socratic view of wonder as the 'beginnings of philosophy'.

The strengths – and the political shortcomings – of Heidegger's 'wonder at the ordinary' were discussed by Hannah Arendt. In an essay marking his eightieth birthday, she expressed some ambivalence about the approach to philosophical thinking that he developed around this version of wonder. While welcoming the reconnection with Socratic 'beginnings', Arendt took the theme in another direction. In *The Life of the Mind*, she presented wonder – in its capacity to confront unexamined opinion – as having a liberating effect on the faculty of judgement, which she spoke of as 'the most political of man's mental abilities'. In linking wonder with both imagination and judgement, Arendt allowed it to reconnect in a new way to ancient wonder – to the old Socratic idea of the philosopher as 'gadfly', criticising the unexamined assumptions of a society.

The role of philosophy in social critique has been given new life in Jacques Derrida's analyses of contemporary cultural and political issues, especially in the close readings of philosophical and literary texts offered in his posthumously published seminars. In *The Beast and the Sovereign*, he explored the idea of 'singularity' in relation to sovereignty, to the death penalty and, more generally, to death itself.

Derrida does not discuss wonder explicitly in these textual readings. Yet his treatment of the ancient idea of *aporia* – the condition in which the perplexed mind comes to a halt with no clear path to follow – is rich with the philosophical history of wonder. It opens up alternative possibilities for reconnecting with the old Socratic ideal of a kind of thinking that 'begins in wonder'.

There are also some important affinities between Derrida's treatment of *singularity* and Spinoza's analysis of wonder. Reading Derrida against the background of the philosophical history of wonder – and in turn looking back at that history through Derrida's insights – can help us better understand contemporary predicaments of wonder. Chapter 6, 'Derrida on *Aporia*, Time and Mortality', explores those connections, focusing especially on Derrida's treatment of the *aporia* arising in relation to the thought of death.

Derrida's reflections on *singularity* and *aporia* in *The Beast and the Sovereign* lead also to some provocative suggestions about stupidity and its connections with philosophy. He associates the philosopher's persistence in asking questions – which of course goes back to its ancient connections with Socratic wonder – with susceptibility to a form of stupidity, captured in the French term *bêtise*. The connotations of that term suggest at least a temporary state of lack in relation to distinctively human rational capacities. Derrida facetiously – but also perceptively – pursues this theme by following some remarks by Gilles Deleuze on *bêtise* down 'the path of Flaubert'.

Discomfort with uncertainty can readily prompt a resort to what Flaubert called 'received opinions' – spurious certainties which debilitate the life of the mind, hardening the spontaneity of thought. Chapter 8, 'Political Wonder and Social Critique', aims to apply insights from the philosophical history of wonder to the critique of aspects of current political debates. Much of what passes for debate in those contexts depends on the circulation of deadening repetitions, which take on the character of established certainties.

One trajectory for this exercise in bringing the philosophical history of wonder to bear on current debates runs from Spinoza's treatment of collective imagination, through more recent notions of 'social imaginaries', to models for the demystification of recurring political narratives. Another trajectory runs from Arendt's observations on Socratic wonder to her appropriation of Kant in her *Lectures on Kant's Political Philosophy*, where she gives more content to her earlier observations about judgement as the 'most political' of human faculties. The chapter brings those two trajectories together in an examination of the current state of political debate on asylum seekers and refugee policy, drawing on Arendt's own treatment of the issue.

Through its associations with awe, wonder has had close relations with religion. The final chapter addresses the implications for wonder of the changing position of religion in secular societies. Does wonder itself change under conditions of secular modernity – in the lack of generally accepted belief in a supernatural realm which suffuses the natural world? Do changing attitudes to the idea of transcendence affect the experience of wonder – or is it just that wonder ceases to be directed towards a realm of supposedly transcendent objects? Here again, the history of ideas of the sublime is central for understanding the conceptual issues at stake.

Jean-François Lyotard, in his *Lessons on the Analytic of the Sublime*, has offered a close reading of crucial passages in Kant's *Critique of Judgement*. Like Deleuze's interpretation of Kant, which is discussed in Chapter 4, Lyotard's reading emphasises Kant's description of an intensely emotional struggle between rival faculties of the mind, each straining to their limits. There are, however, important additional insights which arise from his illuminating discussion.

INTRODUCTION

The language of Kant's 'Analytic of the Sublime' can sound like that of religious experience. Yet Kant repudiated *transcendent* objects of knowledge, casting his own project, rather, as understanding the *transcendental* conditions of human thought. While rejecting knowledge of the supernatural, the Kantian sublime nonetheless evokes its presence. Lyotard's reading emphasises those aspects of the Kantian sublime that foreshadowed – and facilitated – the transition to Romanticism, while also helping explain the continued appeal of elements of the feeling of the sublime for contemporary consciousness.

Human beings will continue to wonder, regardless of what philosophers say about it – or of whether they say anything about it at all. Yet the changing preoccupations of philosophy do reflect – and can sometimes even influence – broader cultural attitudes. What then does it mean to talk, in a philosophical context, of 'reclaiming' wonder? It can suggest an exercise of the kind conducted most explicitly by Heidegger, and, in a different way, by Arendt: reconnecting with insights about wonder from the history of philosophy, and restating them in a new context. It can also mean to *claim back* a territory that has been ceded – in this case, the colonisation of wonder by the fascinations of the sublime.

Reclaiming wonder can also mean something more directly political: a concern with strategies of resistance to the circulation of spurious certainties, which would have us ignore the crucial space between 'knowing' and 'not-knowing' – the space where what Arendt called 'engaged thinking' can occur. This book argues a case for a renewed sense of wonder – reconnected with its political history – to play a role in contemporary social critique. It aims to show that wonder can have political significance, helping to break impasses in debates polarised by a clash of competing narratives.

Although this book considers various strands in the philosophical history of wonder, it does not aim to provide an exhaustive account of that history. Rather, it focuses on particular intellectual episodes that can illuminate what has become of wonder, and how it might be revived or revitalised. My project in reclaiming wonder has also a subsidiary objective: to bring the largely neglected philosophy of Spinoza into the present, as something more than the supposed beginnings of a 'Romantic' sensibility – a frame of mind which, though it still lingers, has by now perhaps outlived the philosophical foundations which once sustained it.

It would be presumptuous for contemporary philosophers to claim a revitalised, politically oriented wonder as a development distinctively associated with their own modes of intellectual inquiry – even if they had any desire to do so. Yet there are ways in which an understanding of the philosophical history of wonder can fruitfully be brought to bear on current issues and predicaments. The book concludes with some reflections on the future of wonder and the role it might continue to play – once it is more clearly understood – in the collective life of the mind.

1

Pause for Thought: Plato and Aristotle on Wonder

The idea of philosophy as having special connections with wonder is an old one. It is not forgotten; yet, though often cited, it receives little consideration or conscious emulation. The idea was powerfully and evocatively expressed in Plato's famous description of Socrates' philosophical initiation of the boy Theaetetus in the Dialogue which bears his name. There, wondering is presented as an experience which is indicative of a cast of mind that marks a potential philosopher: 'This is where philosophy begins and nowhere else.'[1] The young Theaetetus' proneness to wonder makes him an ideal candidate to begin learning from Socrates the art of philosophical questioning.

Socratic Wonder

What is noteworthy about the beautifully crafted exposition of the connections between wonder and philosophical thinking in the *Theaetetus* is that the condition it portrays is not just that of an interest in finding answers to difficult questions. The topic under discussion is the very nature of knowledge. To pursue it philosophically, Socrates must first inculcate in the boy a distinctive mental condition. This wonder, in which philosophy begins, is an intense emotional experience. To describe it, Plato has Socrates draw on a range of metaphors which initially seem inconsistent. On the one hand, the boy's puzzlement in the face of Socrates' questioning brings the activity of thinking to a complete standstill. Yet that apparent immobility is also turmoil. Theaetetus reports: 'I often wonder like mad what these things can mean; sometimes when I'm looking at them I begin to feel quite giddy' (155c; p. 277).

The tensions between metaphors of *stasis* and of turmoil recur throughout the history of the philosophical understanding of wonder. On the one hand, there is the image of a mind transfixed – 'wonderstruck'. On the other, there is what seems an equally appropriate image of a kind of mental restlessness – of a mind wandering, uncertain of its bearings. We can think of wonder as frozen paralysis, but also as restless vacillation. To Theodorus, the boy's mentor in mathematics, Plato gives the articulation of a metaphor which points to a possible reconciliation of that apparent conflict in the experience of wonder between motion and rest. Theaetetus, he says, approaches his studies in a way reminiscent of 'the quiet flow of a stream of oil' (144b; pp. 261–2).

The model of philosophical thinking that emerges in the *Theaetetus* is strikingly different from some common assumptions about how it is best done. What the Dialogue enacts is not a transcending of emotion in favour of contrasted processes of rational thought. Theaetetus continues to 'wonder like mad', but he comes to a better reflective understanding of his states of wonder, and hence to a deeper appreciation of the intellectual character Socrates attributes to the ideal philosopher.

It becomes clear that the art of thinking which Socrates teaches – unlike mathematics, which is Theodorus' area of expertise – is not meant to lead to definitive conclusions. The aim is to teach Theaetetus a kind of thinking which originates in perplexity. Rather than relieving that condition, Socrates' enactment of intellectual 'midwifery' – as he calls his art – both transforms and intensifies it. Theaetetus, in having his nascent thoughts brought to birth, comes to an understanding of his own bewilderment, rather than leaving it behind in a new found certainty. He comes to an understanding and acceptance of his own ongoing *lack* of knowledge.

Plato makes it clear that there are lessons to be drawn from this exercise, not only about its explicit topic – the nature of knowledge – but also about the spirit in which philosophical thinking should be pursued. Concluding the initiation, Socrates assures Theaetetus: 'If ever in the future you should attempt to conceive or should succeed in conceiving other theories, they will be better ones as a result of this enquiry.' In consequence, his companions will find him gentler and less tiresome, more modest, not thinking that he knows what he does not know. This, Socrates insists, is 'all my art can achieve – nothing more' (210c; pp. 350–1).

Where does this leave the consideration of the state of wonder from which the exercise began? We are to understand that Theaetetus is now a better knower, because he no longer thinks of himself as knowing things that he in fact does not know. A resolve to avoid premature commitment to putative knowledge is for Socrates the mark of a philosophical cast of mind. The *Theaetetus* remains a legendary modelling of the education of a young mind into philosophy as a specific form of theoretical inquiry – relentlessly rigorous and adversarial in its persistent questioning mode. Yet we miss the full import of what Plato has Socrates teach Theaetetus if we ignore the origins of that process in wonder. The boy's philosophical initiation involves inducing in him those states of bewilderment which excite and attract him – states in which the mind is brought to a temporary impasse, not knowing where to move. The wonder enacted here is not just a state of excitement accompanying the acquisition of new knowledge. It also has a distinctive connection with the recognition of not-knowing.

The setting that Plato gives the Dialogue is important here; and so too is its positioning in relation to his other Socratic Dialogues. This one ends with Socrates going off to face the charge of 'corrupting youth'. The outcome of that charge will of course be the sentencing of Socrates to death, the story of which is not told here. The *Theaetetus* dramatises Socrates' allegedly subversive activity; but to see what gives it that political edge we must see it in the context of his responses to the charges against him, which are treated in other Dialogues, especially in the earlier *Apology*. Following the story there, we see Socrates, in his self-defence, offer his own account of his educative role. It is, among other things, a fascinating treatment of the social significance of wonder as a central element in the ideal philosophical life.

In this fuller picture, wonder, as well as initiating theoretical inquiry into the natures of things, can also be the beginnings of political awareness. We are thrown into the perplexity of wonder when our established beliefs and habitual expectations are shaken – when things long taken for granted are exposed to challenge. Plato presents Socrates as well aware of this. His efforts to elicit wonder are not designed just to advance theoretical knowledge; they are also oriented towards a broader idea of social critique as a collective good. Socrates warns his accusers that, if he is put to death, they will not easily find anyone to replace the valuable social role he is playing. In a famous metaphor to describe that role, he insists that – rather than corrupting the young – he is arousing the city as if it were a great and noble, but sluggish, horse which he needs to bring to its senses by acting like a gadfly. He never ceases, he says, from thus settling on men – rousing, exhorting and reproaching the intellectually drowsy.

The role of wonder in arousing uncritical minds to engage in social critique, which Plato has Socrates emphasise in the *Apology*, is not sharply separated out from its role in initiating theoretical inquiry, which is central to the *Theaetetus*. In the later Dialogue, the state of intellectual agitation is associated with the desire for a more complete understanding of the nature of knowledge. Yet the emotions attending the sense of wonder, and the associated desire for knowledge, are constant throughout Plato's Dialogues. He has Socrates appropriate to his version of intellectual inquiry the aura of mystery and awe associated with gods and omens.

The Dialogues contain allusions to intimations of bizarre mysteries; to the consulting of oracles; to inner voices, sometimes heard in a trance. Socrates is of course not presented as endorsing such conditions as reliable sources of revealed truth. Yet the references to them are not incidental. They fill out the picture of a complex inner life, in which strategies of rational thought interact with volatile emotion. They also provide insights into the ways in which familiar beliefs and social practices, which are not notable for their rationality, could be transformed into the distinctive Socratic approach to knowing and to not-knowing.

In one of Plato's later Dialogues, the *Symposium*, Socrates gathers with friends to discuss the nature of love. His late arrival is reported as due to his having fallen into one of his trances — states of immobilisation in which he does not stir when called. In the same Dialogue, the Socratic version of wisdom is dramatised by association with stories of divine revelation and intercession. Socrates' own speech on love is offered as having been communicated to him by the wise woman, Diotima of Mantinea. His carefully reasoned contribution is thus framed by a fiction of mysteries imparted by a priestess, who has been commonly talked of as in possession, not only of wisdom, but of magical powers — including an alleged intervention into natural events to delay the onset of plague in Athens.

There are implicit evocations of mysteries and oracles also in the twists and turns of Socrates' speech of self-defence in the *Apology*. He has been accused of disdaining the city's customary gods in favour of alien new divinities. In response, he insists that he has carried out his duties as a citizen who pays appropriate respect to the gods. Socrates claims that this respect has even extended to observing local practices in relation to the consulting of oracles. He cunningly observes that, after all, his own wisdom has been attested by the oracle's pronouncement that Socrates is the wisest of men. His appeal to authority is of course ironic. Plato's audience knows that the wisdom of Socrates is to be understood as grounded in the cultivation of a different kind of wonder from the mysteries which find expression through the local oracles. Yet this Socrates does not hesitate to appropriate to his own ends the pronouncements which the oracle has allegedly made about him.

Socrates goes on to give his own subtle and instructive twist to the interpretation of the oracle. Its declaration becomes the impetus for him to reflect sceptically on the putative wisdom of men in general. The oracle, he insists, merely took him as an example — as if it were saying to men: those who are the wisest among you are like Socrates in knowing that in very truth your wisdom is worth nothing at all. While his critics have accused him of corrupting youth, he has in fact been busy with a divine purpose. He has gone about showing men that, though they thought they were wise, they in fact were not so. Far from showing impiety towards the gods, Socrates continues, his purpose has been to honour them. All philosophers have been accused of teaching people to abandon the old beliefs in the gods. Yet his own intent has not been to convey any impious 'new knowledge'. It has been, on the contrary, to convince people that they know nothing.

In his self-defence, Socrates also talks here of a personal *daimon* – a cautionary 'divine sign' which has guided him from childhood: a kind of voice which whenever he hears it always turns him back from something that he was going to do, but never urges him to act. Again, there is an important rhetorical twist in Socrates' appeal to this mysterious intervention. Omens and oracles usually function to resolve situations of uncertainty. Socrates in contrast insists that his own 'divine sign' is not an authoritative source of knowledge. He refers to it in a context where he is expressing his commitment to the rigorous testing of knowledge claims. His *daimon* speaks to him, but there is no definitive interpretation of what it says. Its warnings are not a substitute for his own thinking. On the contrary, this inner voice cautions him to think for himself; it demands of him a readiness to explore possibilities.

Socrates' warning inner voice is associated with deliberation rather than certainty. Its role is to bring about a reflective pause in thinking. Here again, we are in the territory of wonder – construed as a hiatus in thought. Socrates invokes accustomed associations of wonder with awe and mystery in articulating his own notion of an attentiveness that underpins both thought and action. The voice of the *daimon* imposes a stillness, which issues in an enriched intellectual activity.

Socratic wonder brings thought to a halt. In confronting the unknown – bewildered at conflicting possibilities – the mind finds itself with nowhere to move. In the *Apology*, Socrates plays upon this theme to cleverly turn his listeners' attention to the consideration of the Dialogue's most important theme – the mind-stopping contemplation of mortality. It is impossible, he observes, to know what, if anything, lies beyond death; hence, it is also impossible to know whether death is really a good or an evil. He goes on to turn the complexities of un-knowing, in relation to death, into a further shrewd argumentative move in his self-defence. If – faced with the consequence of his own death – he were to abandon his allegedly corrupting activities, he would in effect be repudiating the oracle which has declared him wise. Moreover, to cease his educative activities out of fear of death would itself be a major instantiation of wrongly thinking himself to be wise. For it would be to suppose that he knows that his death would be an evil.

Socrates goes on to generalise the argument beyond his own case. For all that we know, death may in fact be our greatest good; yet we foolishly fear it, as if we know quite well that it is the greatest of evils. 'And what is this but that shameful ignorance of thinking that we know what we do not know?'[2] Drawing together the threads of his argument, he suggests that the very absence of the voice of his *daimon* in his current situation is itself a wonderful thing. For it indicates that he is right in not thinking of death as an evil. The prophetic sign has been with him all through his life until now, opposing him in quite small matters, if he was not going to act rightly. It has often stopped him in the very act of speaking. Hence, he reasons, what is happening to him now, as he faces death, must be something good. 'And those of us who think that death is an evil must needs be mistaken.'[3] At the end of his defence, Socrates seems more inclined to think of death as a good than as an evil. However, he insists that he knows neither that it is good nor that it is evil. What matters is to avoid claiming knowledge which he does not have.

The treatment of wonder as the beginnings of philosophy; the idea of wisdom as a kind of not-knowing; the metaphor of the gadfly for the philosopher's role in social critique; the centrality of the contemplation of death in philosophical self-understanding – all these evocative and interconnected themes cluster around the Socratic idea of wonder. They have made Plato's Socratic Dialogues legendary in the evolving history of the idea of the philosopher. What can we now make of these old connections between philosophy and wonder? Could, or should, anything of it be salvaged to yield a plausible model of philosophical thinking worthy of contemporary emulation?

Plato's imaginative reconstructions offer a contentious picture of the disruptive activities of the historical Socrates. The positive image of the philosopher as a gadfly – intent on constructive social critique of the powerful – can be countered by an alternative narrative of a mischievous dissident intent on social destabilisation.[4] Plato had his own ideas, too, about the social role of the philosopher. In the *Republic* he sketched the disturbing figure of the authoritarian 'philosopher king', whose penetrating insight into the true natures of things is supposed to underpin the right ordering of society. The fluidity of Socratic wonder gives way to something more rigid when Plato speaks in his own voice.

Yet something of that Socratic fluidity – of the celebration of not-knowing – has persisted in the understanding of wonder.

Metaphors connecting it with mental motion and rest – turmoil and tranquillity – recur throughout the history of western philosophy. Later we will see some more recent philosophers attempting to revive something of what was distinctive in Socratic wonder. First, however, let us see how the philosophical understanding of wonder unfolded.

Aristotelian Wonder

Aristotle continued the theme of philosophy's origins in wonder. In the *Metaphysics*, he says that philosophy began when human beings wondered – at first about easily resolved questions, then advancing little by little to state difficulties about 'the greater matters, e.g. about the phenomena of the moon and those of the sun and of the stars, and about the genesis of the universe'.[5] These passages also evoke the idea of a state of mental agitation, which the wondering mind seeks to resolve. Aristotle describes it in terms of a kind of wavering or vacillation, reflecting a lack of precision – a kind of hovering between not-knowing and knowing. That mental wavering, he suggests, gives philosophy – the love of wisdom – something in common with myth. For lovers of myth are also, in a sense, lovers of wisdom, since myths are composed of things not completely understood – of wonders.

The relationships between philosophy, myth and poetry had been a vexed issue for Plato. In the *Republic*, he presented philosophy and literature as at odds: the poets are untrustworthy as guides to truth. Yet his own works – including the *Republic* itself – are full of myths and metaphors. Aristotle's treatment of wonder acknowledges the affinities between the love of myth and the love of philosophy. He took further than Plato himself had done an aspect of the *Republic*'s treatment of the 'divided soul': the significant role of desire in the operations of the mind. Aristotle stresses that the 'not-knowing' associated with wonder is not just an acknowledged absence of knowledge; it brings with it an intense desire to understand.

In his treatment of wonder, Aristotle was not responding directly to Plato; yet his remarks serve to refine Plato's metaphors of minds in motion. The wondering mind passes from ignorance to knowledge, but it is not a direct flight. The restlessness which Plato had evocatively presented as a state of giddiness – 'wondering like mad' – is redescribed to emphasise the affective dimensions of wonder. The wondering mind is not just in a state of disoriented agitation. It yearns for relief from its own bitter-sweet perplexity. These connections with desire give Aristotle's version of the thinking inspired by wonder an orientation that will prove crucial in later developments. The thinking which begins in wonder is distinctive in having as its rationale the pursuit of knowledge for its own sake. It has no end or purpose, other than the alleviation of wonder. Other kinds of thought may be more useful, he says, yet none is better. This emphasis on its end-state has a consequence which we will later see shape attitudes to wonder in ways that go beyond Aristotle's own formulation of the point.

Knowledge driven by wonder, Aristotle observes, must, in a sense, end in something that is the opposite of its beginning. Wonder involves a transition – an alleviation of unease or dissatisfaction. We start by wondering at things being as they are, but 'we must end in the contrary and, according to the proverb, the better state'.[6] In other words, wonder gives way to the superior end-state of increased knowledge. There is an appearance of ambiguity here between two senses of 'end': as teleological finality – direction towards a desired goal – and, on the other hand, as cessation. Yet both senses are important to Aristotle's point. In the context of his broader treatment of acts and processes, wonder and its 'end' are conceptually interdependent. They are not separable in any way that would allow wonder to be construed as a state to be avoided or minimised by those intent on seeking the end-state – knowledge. Wonder involves a dissatisfaction which the inquiring mind desires to remedy, but that initial dissatisfaction is essential to reaching the goal. For Aristotle it is not an intrusive, vexatious irritant from which the mind should seek liberation in order to attain its own true good.

Aristotle elaborates the affective dimensions of wonder in Book I of his *Rhetoric*, emphasising its connections with desire and pleasure. He says there that learning and wondering at things are both as a rule pleasant. Wondering implies 'the desire of learning, so that the object of wonder is an object of desire; while in learning one is brought into one's natural condition'.[7] This approach to wonder gives new content to old metaphors of minds in motion. Rather than being just restless fluctuation, wonder comes to be seen as purposeful, end-directed intellectual activity.

Later in Aristotelian thought, St Thomas Aquinas refined that teleological emphasis by relating wonder directly to the mind's yearning for knowledge. The wondering mind longs for understanding, as a state of rest which it perceives as its own good. Elaborating, in his *Summa Theologiae*, the Aristotelian treatment of the mind's activities, he says, in the first part of Part II, at Q32, Art. 8, that wonder is a kind of desire for knowledge, arising from the fact that we see effects without their causes – or from the fact that those causes exceed our capacity to know. Wonder involves a lack of knowledge, but that lack is not a mere absence. Aquinas saw wonder as itself a cause of pleasure, in so far as it is accompanied by the hope of reaching the desired knowledge of the object. All things that give rise to wonder, he says, are pleasurable; and even those things that are not pleasurable in themselves become so if their rarity gives rise to wonder.

Knowing and Not-Knowing

The Platonic and the Aristotelian treatments of wonder will play out differently in their subsequent histories. Socratic wonder will be associated more explicitly with the search for wisdom; it matters because it is the 'beginnings' of good living. Theaetetus is initiated, not just into a method for reaching knowledge, but into a long process of becoming wise. Aristotelian wonder, in contrast, will reverberate in later philosophical preoccupations with the right methods for acquiring theoretical knowledge. It is, however, important to remember their original shared concern with the place of wonder in living well.

Despite their different emphases, both Plato and Aristotle presented wonder as a positive feature of mental activity. Whatever unease or restlessness it might involve, it is ultimately of great importance to the mind's well-being. Their concern with wonder is encompassed by consideration of the requirements for a good human life. What matters here is not just knowledge as end-state or product. The processes of coming to know — the mind's activity — are crucial to living well. On Plato's approach, this means that the recognition of 'not-knowing' is no less important than the process of coming to know.

The idealisation of 'not-knowing' is a strong — and elusive — theme throughout Plato's Socratic Dialogues. Clearly, what is being extolled is not mere ignorance. Socratic not-knowing is not a deprivation of the good that resides in knowledge. It is, rather, an acknowledged state of ongoing lack of knowledge in the midst of knowing. In the Aristotelian treatment of wonder, there is no equivalent celebration of not-knowing. Aristotle says that the end-state of knowing is 'more noble' than the beginning of the process of coming to know. Yet it is a superiority that acknowledges the wholeness of the process that begins in wonder – the superiority of the 'end', which gives meaning and purpose to the beginning. The Aristotelian celebration of the completed process is articulated within the context of a strong emphasis on the unified activity of the mind in moving from not-knowing to knowing – and on the emotional aspects of that transition: its connections with pleasure and desire.

Despite the greater 'nobility' of the end-state, there is in the Aristotelian treatment of wonder no suggestion – or even possibility – of denigrating the wonder that begins the process of coming to know. It is the whole process that is emphasised. Its 'beginning' is not treated with suspicion, even if its 'end' is inevitably the better state. It would not make sense within this unity of 'coming to know' to treat wonder as a possible impediment to knowing.

In both the Socratic and the Aristotelian approaches to wonder, there is thus a recognition of a unity of knowing and not-knowing, which can seem strange from later perspectives. It does not come easily for modern minds, attuned to equating knowledge with the benefits of *certainty*, to see 'not-knowing' as something positive. The wisdom that Plato had Socrates inculcate in the boy Theaetetus is not scepticism – in either its ancient or its modern forms. Theaetetus will go on seeking to know. Yet, the goal of Socratic questioning is not an ultimate gaining of knowledge which cannot be further questioned. Nor can Aristotle's 'nobler' end-state be identified with modern ideals of certainty.

When Descartes in the seventeenth century comes to reflect on what is distinctive in what he sees as the 'passion' of wonder, its status in relation to the mind's activity in reaching knowledge becomes more problematic.

Notes

1 Plato, *Theaetetus*, trans. Margaret Jane Levett, in Myles Burnyeat, ed., *The Theaetetus of Plato* (Indianapolis: Hackett Publishing Company, 1990), 155d, p. 277. Further page references will be given in the main text.
2 Plato, *Apology*, trans. F. J. Church, in *The Trial and Death of Socrates* (London: Macmillan and Co, Ltd, 1952), XVII, 29, p. 57.
3 Plato, *Apology*, XXXI, pp. 75–6.
4 For an interesting discussion of the rival interpretations of the social role of the historical Socrates, see I. F. Stone, *The Trial and Death of Socrates* (London: Pimlico, 1988).
5 Aristotle, *Metaphysics*, trans. W. D. Ross, in Richard McKeon, ed., *The Basic Works of Aristotle* (New York: Random House, 1941); A.2, 982b, p. 692.
6 Aristotle, *Metaphysics*, A.3, 983a17, p. 693.
7 Aristotle, *Rhetoric*, trans. Rhys Roberts, in McKeon, ed., *The Basic Works of Aristotle*, Bk 1, Ch. 11, 1371a31, p. 1365.

2

Passion or Distraction? Descartes and Spinoza on Wonder

Descartes was ambivalent about wonder. Like Plato and Aristotle, he valued it as a stimulus to intellectual inquiry, yet he also saw it as a threat to the advancement of knowledge. In his *Passions of the Soul*, wonder is given the status of a 'primary' passion. Along with love, hatred, desire, joy and sadness, it is simple and irreducible. These primary passions fall directly – without reference to any others – under his general definition of human passions: 'those perceptions, sensations or emotions of the soul which we refer particularly to it, and which are caused, maintained and strengthened by some movement of the spirits'.[1]

Wonder, Mind and Matter

There is something puzzling about the formulation of Descartes' definition of the passions of the soul, which famously elicited Spinoza's derision – as well as the more polite questioning raised by Descartes' friend, Princess Elizabeth, in her insightful correspondence with him. Descartes' treatment of the passions is framed by his notorious treatment of mind and matter as utterly separate kinds of thing. Wonder is for him a state of the soul;

yet its causes are bodily – changes in the 'animal spirits', which he has earlier in the work described as 'extremely small bodies which move very quickly' (Part I, Sec. 10; p. 332). Descartes has here given older metaphors of mental motion a strikingly literal content in terms of the movements of tiny bodies.

From the start, then, Descartes' treatment of wonder raises an issue which will be central to Spinoza's caustic critique of it: the power of small, fast-moving material bodies to bring about changes in a supposedly immaterial soul or mind. There is, on the face of it, something strange about the very idea of a Cartesian 'passion of the soul'. In being 'referred to' an immaterial soul, such states would seem to pertain to it independently of what happens in the separate domain of Cartesian matter. Yet, by Descartes' definition, they are caused and influenced by movements of material things, as well as supposedly belonging to the mind itself. Within this general analysis, he offers as his specific definition of wonder that it is 'a sudden surprise of the soul which brings it to consider with attention the objects that seem to it unusual and extraordinary' (Part II, Sec. 70; p. 353).

For Descartes, wonder is supposed to bring a heightening of the mind's attention under the force of confrontation with the unexpected – an impact that depends on a causal interaction of mind and matter. Spinoza had no problem with wonder being defined in terms of the mind's surprise at strangeness. However, in response to Descartes' account of that surprise, he wryly claimed to be very surprised indeed.

The differences in their accounts of wonder follow on from a deeper disagreement – Spinoza's repudiation of Descartes' views on the nature of the human mind. Whereas for Descartes minds are individual – separately existing – intellectual substances, they are for Spinoza *ideas* of body: modifications of the one unique Substance-or-God, under the *attribute* of thought. Spinoza argues that, because thought and matter are different attributes of Substance, each expressing totally its nature, there can be between them no causal interaction, but only a complete parallelism. The relation between a mind and 'its' body now becomes that of an idea to its object – a relation between modes of Substance under different attributes. However, the disagreements between Spinoza and the Cartesians on wonder are not just reflections of Spinoza's repudiation of what he sees as the mysterious causal interactions between Cartesian minds and matter. There are also some crucial differences more specific to wonder, which illuminate ways in which Descartes' version of it departs from the Platonic and Aristotelian accounts.

Although wonder conforms to Descartes' general causal account of the way passions arise in the soul, he sees it as having a distinctive feature which sets it apart from his other 'primary' passions. Despite being caused by the 'animal spirits' acting on mind, wonder is not accompanied by any 'change in the heart or in the blood' (Part II, Sec. 71; p. 353). That may sound like an incidental physiological observation, but it rests on what Descartes sees as a distinguishing conceptual feature of wonder. It arises from its special connection with knowledge. Unlike the other 'primary' passions, wonder does not have 'good or evil' as its object. It is not directed to our practical dealings with the world. Rather than being concerned with securing our well-being, wonder aims only at knowledge of the things which initiate it.

This marks an important break from the Platonic and Aristotelian treatments of wonder. Plato's reconstruction of Socratic wonder, as we have seen, dramatised its role in the good human life – its connections with the wise recognition of not-knowing – as well as its significance in stimulating theoretical inquiry into the natures of things. The Aristotelian approach was centred on wonder's role in attaining the goal of knowledge, rather than the Socratic ideal of acknowledged not-knowing; yet it still celebrated wonder's role in the purposes and pleasures of the well-lived life. Descartes' treatment of wonder, in contrast, invokes a distinction between the theoretical and the practical. For him wonder has a more explicitly theoretical orientation – towards certainty, rather than towards a practical concern with what is good or evil for human knowers. It is with regard to this putative special orientation towards theoretical inquiry that Descartes sees wonder as falling short.

Although Descartes' definitions insist on this sharp distinction between wonder and other passions, his general descriptions of the lived experience of wonder are more nuanced. Wonder, he says, typically occurs in conjunction with other passions – adding to their turbulence. Indeed, because surprise is 'proper and peculiar' to it, wonder brings an additional intensity to other passions with which it is joined, creating a propensity to emotional excess (Part II, Sec. 72; pp. 353–4). So, although wonder is of itself directed only towards knowledge, it can nonetheless serve to endanger our practical well-being. By way of illustration, Descartes talks of 'astonishment' as an excess of wonder which, he warns, can immobilise us in our efforts to acquire knowledge. Such intellectual paralysis makes knowledge of the object impossible; hence astonishment 'can never be other than bad' (Part II, Sec. 73; p. 354).

Wonder thus occupies an ambiguous place among Descartes' 'passions of the soul'. Although he says that it is not directed towards what is either good or bad for the soul, he regards it, not only as dangerous, but also as useful – in strengthening in us thoughts which it is good to have. It is useful — at any rate to begin with — in the gaining of knowledge. Because we feel wonder in the face of what appears unusual, it acts a stimulus to learn and retain in memory things we did not previously know. Hence, he says, those who are not prone to wonder are usually very ignorant. Yet, he also insists, more often we wonder too much rather than too little — readily becoming lost in astonishment at things that do not really merit much consideration. In Plato's Dialogues, Socrates' recurring states of immobilised wondering were treated with bemused respect. For Descartes, it seems, rather, that our becoming like statues through excessive wonder is a greater risk to our well-being than that posed by ignorance resulting from wondering too little.

Despite its potential benefits, wonder is for Descartes a risky venture. Aristotle suggested that it was 'less noble' than the end-state in which it finds completion. Descartes goes further, treating it as a definite threat to knowledge. Underlying these differences in attitude are different ways of conceptualising wonder. Descartes' distrust is fed by his image of the mind as immobilised like a statue. The more positive Aristotelian evaluation of wonder rests on thinking of it rather as an active yearning for rest in knowledge, as a desired end-state. Moreover, on that approach, wonder was not just a pre-condition for knowing; it remained an inseparable aspect of the ongoing process of gaining it.

The crucial contrast here is that Descartes thinks of wonder as a condition separate from knowing, and potentially at odds with it: 'Therefore, although it is good to be born with some inclination to wonder, since it makes us disposed to acquire scientific knowledge, yet after acquiring such knowledge we must attempt to free ourselves from this inclination as much as possible' (Part II, Sec. 76; p. 355). He has said that wonder, unlike his other 'primary passions', is directed only towards knowledge — not to more practical concerns with living well. Yet he also says that it is potentially a threat to knowledge. It is supposed to be all about knowledge; yet it does not ultimately serve us well in acquiring it.

Descartes' departures from the Aristotelian approach to wonder rest also on an emphasis on a construct which is not present in the ancient treatments of wonder, and which will be explicitly repudiated by Spinoza — the faculty of will. For Descartes the exercise of a virtuous will is the remedy for excessive states of passion, including unwarranted wonder. It is the will that allows us to set aside wonder and make good its absence through 'a special state of reflection and attention', which it can always 'impose upon our understanding when we judge the matter before us to be worth serious consideration' (Part II, Sec. 76, p. 355).

To some extent, inappropriate wonder ceases of its own accord; as we become more used to things, we find them less novel. However, Descartes saw that natural diminution of wonder as needing external assistance from an exercise of the will. Without the 'remedy' the will provides, we can gradually become so full of wonder that things of no importance are just as apt to arrest our attention as those whose investigation is more useful to us. The uncorrected habit of wonder can thus prolong the troubles of 'those afflicted with blind curiosity, i.e. those who seek out rarities simply in order to wonder at them and not in order to know them' (Part II, Sec. 78; p. 356). Gaping at strange 'wonders' can all too easily become a substitute for genuine understanding, which demands sustained intellectual activity.

Descartes' reservations about wonder are, in their intellectual and cultural context, not far-fetched. His warnings of the mental paralysis that it might induce did answer to some aspects of the seventeenth-century fascination with strange objects. In their comprehensive study of the topographies of wonder in western intellectual history, *Wonders and the Orders of Nature*, Lorraine Daston and Katharine Park give an intriguing account of the popularity of the strange collections assembled in 'cabinets of wonder' throughout the seventeenth and eighteenth centuries. These esoteric collections went beyond the previously common, specialised, professional collections of anomalous natural objects. The more modern collections typically brought art and nature together:

> precious materials, exotica and antiquities, specimens of exquisite workmanship, and natural and artificial oddities – all crammed together in order to dazzle the onlooker. If each object by itself elicited wonder, all of them densely arrayed floor to ceiling or drawer upon drawer could only amplify the visitor's gasp of mingled astonishment and admiration.[2]

It is a description which fits well with Descartes' criticism of gaping wonder at the unusual – a poor substitute for the pursuit of genuine understanding. Yet his appeal to the ministrations of a virtuous will to control the excesses of wonder yielded, as Spinoza saw it, no less absurd a model of the mind's efforts to know.

The Surprise of Wonder

Echoing familiar motifs in the Platonic and Aristotelian accounts of wonder, Spinoza, like Descartes, centres his treatment of wonder on the idea of a pause in the mind's activity in the face of something unfamiliar. However he draws very different conclusions from that hiatus in activity. In the *Ethics*, he defines affects – of which passions are a subclass – in terms of transitions in activity: 'affections of the Body by which the Body's power of acting is increased or diminished, aided or restrained, and at the same time, the ideas of those affections'.[3] For Spinoza, affects involve mental movement – a transition in degree of activity. Hence, since wonder involves *stasis* – a cessation of activity – it cannot be considered an affect. Thus wonder, which Descartes had treated as a 'primary' passion, becomes for Spinoza no passion at all. Its presence nonetheless haunts his treatment of the emotions which he regards as genuine affects. Wonder plays a central role in the formation, and transformation, of a wide range of emotions. Despite not being itself an affect, it is for Spinoza crucial to the emotional aspects of the life of the mind – both individually and collectively.

Against the background of the differences with Descartes in regard to mind, matter and general definitions of the passions, Spinoza's treatment of wonder is startling. Wonder now enters into the relationship between a mind and its body. If a mind is struck by wonder, then that is to say that the apprehension of its own body – the body of which it is the idea – becomes something at which it wonders. Spinoza's initial observations about this aspect of wonder are deceptively uncontroversial. 'The Body itself, simply from the laws of its own nature, can do many things which its Mind wonders at' (Part III, Scholium to Proposition 2; p. 495). With that much, Descartes could readily agree. In the *Passions of the Soul*, he himself offers numerous accounts of what bodies can do autonomously, without the intervention of mind. However, Spinoza goes on to challenge belief in the very possibility of mind–body interaction, which was central to the Cartesian treatment of the passions:

> No one knows how, or by what means, the Mind moves the body . . . So it follows that when men say that this or that action of the Body arises from the Mind, which has dominion over the Body, they do not know what they are saying, and they do nothing but confess, in fine-sounding words, that they are ignorant of the true cause of that action, and that they do not wonder at it.

For Spinoza the state of wonder reaches into the very core of mind's relations with the body of which it is the idea. In mischievous tones, he appeals to the mind's wonder at the capacities of bodies in order to ridicule what he sees as incongruities in Descartes' analysis of wonder – and of the passions in general – in terms of mind–body interaction. His critique of Descartes' specific account of wonder is both subtle and sarcastic – at once playful and devastating. It is a sustained reflection on the pause in mental activity which – as he agrees with Descartes – is central to wonder. For both of them, wonder indicates a lack of knowledge; but Spinoza has found a way to turn that familiar point against the Cartesians. He argues that, if minds are – as the Cartesians suppose – separately existing individual substances, causally interacting with matter, then the nature of the passions, and how the will can 'remedy' their excess, must remain mysterious.

Spinoza cunningly suggests that the minds of his opponents are so habituated to accepting the mysterious that their acknowledged not-knowing does not even trigger wonder. His ridicule of Descartes' alleged lack of wonder at the strangeness of his account of the passions is an *ad hominem* jibe. In the Preface to Part III of the *Ethics*, he observes that 'the celebrated Descartes' tries to show how the mind has absolute power over its affects; but in fact he 'shows nothing but the cleverness of his understanding' (p. 492).

He returns to the attack in the Preface to Part V, presenting Descartes' lack of wonder at his own outrageous theory as itself an object of wonder. After summarising Descartes' description of the will acting as a causal force to control the soul's passions, he says that, had that account not been so subtle, he could not have believed it had been propounded by so great a man. He 'cannot wonder enough', he says, that a philosopher of Descartes' calibre – one who has so often censured the Scholastic philosophers for wishing to explain obscure things by occult qualities – 'should assume a Hypothesis more occult than any occult quality' (p. 596).

On Spinoza's own account, it comes naturally to the mind to wonder at the body of which it is the idea. For the striving to understand that body – and through it the rest of the world – is crucial to the mind's very existence. For Aristotle, wonder was an expression of the mind's striving for understanding. That striving was for him a purposeful intellectual activity, directed towards knowledge as its end. In Aquinas' philosophy, that intellectual effort became more explicitly 'a certain sort of desire'. For Spinoza it becomes the mind's *conatus* – an inherent striving which he identifies with the very essence of an individual mind. The mind struggles to continue in existence as an ever more adequate understanding of body, of which it is the idea.

All this puts Spinoza's approach to wonder on a different trajectory from Descartes' appeal to an extraneous will as the remedy for its excesses. On the Aristotelian approach, where wonder was seen as an expression of the mind's natural desire for knowledge, no such appeal to will as a causal force was necessary. For Spinoza, too, there is no need – or even possibility – of appeal to a will. For him, the role that Descartes gives the will in controlling wonder is played by the mind's inherent effort to understand. That effort requires, not just an exercise of reason, but its interaction with imagination. It is here that we see most clearly the novelty – and the long-term significance – of Spinoza's way of construing wonder.

The key to his transformation of wonder is his elaboration of the theme of surprise at the unfamiliar. He gives content to that old understanding of wonder through a notion of *singularity*. Surprise remains central in Spinoza's account, but is now differently construed. The emphasis shifts from Descartes' evocation of a psychological state of stunned immobility to a more formal consideration of relations among objects of attention. Here the significance of the role Spinoza gives to imagination in knowledge becomes apparent. In his Definition of the Affects, at the end of Part III of the *Ethics*, he describes it as 'an imagination of a thing in which the Mind remains fixed because this singular imagination has no connection with the others' (p. 532). In wonder, the mind is brought to a standstill by the singularity of an object of attention.

In his general account of knowledge, Spinoza gives imagination the role of bringing things together for comparison. Although not itself a source of adequate knowledge, imagination thus makes possible reason's grasp of what things have in common. It is when the basis for comparison is not apparent that the mind is forced to pause in its contemplation. 'If we have previously seen an object together with others, or we imagine it has nothing but what is common to many things, we shall not consider it so long as one which we imagine to have something singular' (Part III, Proposition 52; p. 523).

In explaining this halt in the mind's operations, Spinoza highlights imagination's easy transitions between similar things: 'When we suppose that we imagine in an object something singular, which we have never seen before, we are only saying that when the Mind considers that object, it has nothing in itself which it is led to consider from considering that. And so it is determined to consider only that.' This focus on singularity is for Spinoza the core of wonder. As he says in the accompanying Scholium, 'This Affection of the Mind, or this imagination of a singular thing, insofar as it is alone in the Mind, is called Wonder' (p. 523). It is a succinct formulation, which brings out what are for Spinoza the limitations and the strengths of the capacity to imagine.

The connections Spinoza forges here between wonder and imagination are grounded in painstaking definitions and deductions. They make for dry reading. Yet they express a conceptual refinement in the understanding of wonder which has far-reaching consequences. The style and tone of his dissection of wonder seem to belong in a different world from the later exultation in the wild and wondrous powers of imagination associated with Romanticism. Yet his treatment of imagination – cerebral though his version of it may sound – makes those later developments possible. Spinoza insists that the imagination does not of itself yield adequate understanding. Yet it is a precondition for knowledge. It is through imagination that the mind is able to retain traces of bodily affections – to have things before it that are no longer actually present. That is what allows reason to grasp what is common to different bodily modifications. So, if wonder brings the exercise of imagination to a halt, the mind's search for commonalities – the cultivation of reason – is also temporarily blocked.

By stressing the connections between wonder and imagination, Spinoza is thus able to give more explicit content to the old idea of wonder as a pause in thought: it is a fixation of the imagination. In explaining his exclusion of wonder from the affects, in the Definitions at the end of Part III of the *Ethics*, he says that, rather than being a transition to greater or less activity, it is a 'distraction of the Mind' – arising not from any positive cause, but only from the fact that there is nothing 'determining the Mind to pass from regarding one thing to thinking of others' (p. 532). Wonder involves a fixity, bringing a halt to the flow of imagination's movement between similarities.

The associations with imagination also allow Spinoza to clarify wonder's collective aspects – its connections with sociability. Those connections become apparent in his treatment of the dynamics of disdain, which he regards as the opposite of wonder. For him, disdain is explained through the influence of minds on one another. It arises in reaction to our initial tendency to seek to emulate the wonder which others direct to an object. We then find, on closer consideration, that we are determined by the thing's presence to think more of the things that are not in the object than of those that are within it (Part III, Scholium to Proposition 52; pp. 523–4). Spinoza's analysis of disdain shows how the singularity of an object of attention can become a point of interaction between imagination, emotion and reason. Confronted with singularity, the mind is prompted to turn towards other things, which it can more readily understand. The initial 'distraction' of unfounded, admiring wonder then turns to disdain.

Spinoza's account of disdain offers an intriguing analysis of the vicissitudes of wonder, which highlights its social dimensions. The mental *stasis* induced by singularity involves a thwarted anticipation – a frustration of expectation. Yet this pause in thought can strengthen understanding rather than diminishing it. Here the mind, striving for understanding – as it must of its nature do – finds itself forced to revise its initial judgement, which was influenced by the positive estimation others have thoughtlessly bestowed on an object. High esteem – where it depends on thoughtless imitation of others – is dispelled under the force of the mind's own efforts to understand.

In the short term, wonder does not always have immediate positive effects. Spinoza acknowledges that it can bring challenges both in theoretical inquiry and in practical affairs. He points out, for example, that 'consternation' – which he defines as wonder aroused by an object we fear – can be a species of cowardice. It is attributed to one whose desire is restrained by wonder at the evil he fears – 'a Fear that keeps a man senseless or vacillating so that he cannot avert the evil' (Part III, Explanation to Definition of the Affects, XLII; p. 540).

These debilitating effects of 'consternation' are similar to those Descartes attributes to 'astonishment'. Yet for Spinoza there is no need to appeal to an extraneous virtuous will to bring a remedy. The mind's stunned apprehension of singularity brings to the striving mind its own restorative return to greater activity. Encountering singularity, the imagination initially finds no room to move. However, having been stopped in its tracks, it resorts to finding less obvious resemblances. Given that the mind of its nature – its *conatus* – strives to persist in understanding, the blocked pathway becomes an impetus to finding alternative ways forward. The mind, temporarily rendered passive by opposing forces, finds its way back to the activity of thought in which its continued existence consists.

There is a lot going on here which depends on a complex and integrated metaphysical system – on Spinoza's treatment of Substance and attributes, and of minds as 'ideas' of body; on his rejection of the will in favour of a rich, but puzzling, concept of *conatus*. For Spinoza, wonder belongs in a non-causal relationship between mind and body. It arises in the mind's initial response to something unfamiliar – something not understood – happening in the body of which it is the idea. This offers a fresh and provocative perspective on the old idea of wonder as the beginnings of philosophical inquiry: a mind responds to the presence of its own body as something which it does not understand, but which it must nonetheless try to understand in order to continue being what it is. For Spinoza wonder is thus necessary for a mind's continued existence. In construing it as the imagination's encounter with unexpected singularity, he has reconfigured its relations with knowledge. Wonder is here seen as inherent in the mind's ongoing striving to better understand body – an effort which brings in turn an ever better understanding of itself.

In Spinoza's philosophy, a mind's efforts to know must begin from its inadequate awareness of the world – and hence of itself. Its knowledge is mediated through a confused conglomerate of bodily affections – the domain of imagination. Yet it is always in principle possible to increase our knowledge through the imagination's power to apprehend resemblances. In contrast, the Cartesians – on Spinoza's scathing account of them – acquiesce in mystery. They do not even wonder at the strangeness of the supposed causal relations between minds and bodies, to which they appeal in explaining our passions – including wonder itself. They lack the self-reflection to realise that their inquiries have come to a premature dead-end. Descartes emphasised the hazards of excessive wonder. Spinoza turns the tables on the Cartesians, suggesting that they do not wonder enough.

Spinoza's emphasis is on the ways in which wonder can coexist with and strengthen our efforts to know. Although it brings the mind to a temporary halt in its attempts to understand itself and the world, wonder is readily redirected at the remarkable capacities of human bodies in interaction with one another. Properly understood, wonder thus enhances the mind's struggle to understand the natural world and its own place in it.

Spinoza's disdain for what he sees as the Cartesians' ready acquiescence in mysteries strikingly enacts his own analysis of disdain. He reports that the high regard in which Descartes is commonly held had at first inclined him to admire Cartesian doctrines; yet admiration turned to disdain on closer examination. Hence his cunning suggestion, in the Preface to Part V of the *Ethics*, that the Cartesians' minds are so habituated to the acceptance of the mysterious that their acknowledged not-knowing does not even trigger wonder.

Spinoza saw the Cartesians' apparent acquiescence in mystery as reflecting a deeply flawed way of thinking – not only of the relations between human minds and bodies, but more generally of the relations between God and the world. Descartes' God was a transcendent Creator, with an omnipotent will, whose ways cannot be fully grasped by human beings. Indeed, Descartes notoriously held that the eternal laws of reason are themselves dependent on the omnipotent divine will. That commitment to divine transcendence of Nature underlies the 'mysteries' of which Spinoza complains in his rejection of Cartesian doctrines.

Descartes himself had repudiated opportunistic appeals to direct divine intervention to explain what happens in the natural world. Yet his God remained in principle capable of interrupting the established order of the world he had made. Spinoza regarded that attitude as reinforcing the acquiescence in mysteries which he saw as preventing the Cartesians from pursuing sustained investigation into things as yet unexplained.

Wonder and Imagination

In his *Theological-Political Treatise*, Spinoza addressed more fully the wider aspects of wonder-inducing encounters with singularity. Here, his treatments of imagination and of religion fill out his observations in the *Ethics* on the social aspects of wonder. What emerges is that wonder is caught up in the powerful interactions between imagination and emotion, which can both unite and divide human beings.

Spinoza argued in the *Ethics* that imagination, though of itself inadequate as a source of knowledge, nonetheless enables and facilitates the operations of reason. In his treatment of prophecies and miracles in the *Theological-Political Treatise*, he offers a fuller and less formalised account of the interactions of intellect, imagination and emotion in the development and sustaining of forms of human sociability. Concern with the wonders narrated in the biblical stories – and with the state of wonder they elicit – is central to that account.

Spinoza sees the biblical narratives as powerful exercises of imagination. They are fictions – inadequate as accounts of what goes on in the natural world. Yet he argues that these stories should be neither condemned for their falsity nor dismissed as useless. Despite their flawed representation of events, they can – when sensibly used – facilitate collective human flourishing. They do not yield knowledge of the natural world, but they are appropriate vehicles for the communication of shared wisdom about how best to live. However, they also become vehicles of superstitions – to the detriment of reason – when their appeal is exploited by untrustworthy theologians, who present themselves as the interpreters of divinely revealed truth. Having used the mysteries narrated in biblical stories to induce intense emotions of hope and fear, they then pose as the authoritative interpreters of those narratives, in order to allay fear and invite hope in ways that reinforce their own power.

Belief in divine revelation – construed literally as the deliverances of an all-powerful, punitive, transcendent being – is for Spinoza a source of pernicious falsehoods. Yet he recognises also the more positive associations of religion with emotions such as joy, love, generosity and awe, which can foster bonds of shared humanity and enrich communal responses to the world. Religious rituals, and the imaginative narratives which sustain them, can play a positive role, contributing to social order and collective well-being – once their putative associations with divinely revealed truth about the world have been repudiated. Spinoza's critique of the biblical accounts of prophecies and miracles is thus not so much a denigration of religion as an attempt to understand its social role – and to expose its misuse by those intent on discrediting, or attempting to suppress, scientific inquiry.

Although Spinoza has been often construed as an enemy of religion, his criticism of it is of a kind very different from those of some of the more zealous atheists of our own time. He rejected the supernatural, and derided superstition. He argued against the encroachment of theologically inspired authorities on scholarly pursuits, and on political life. Yet, like many later Enlightenment thinkers, he aimed to accommodate religion rather than to destroy it. We will see the significance of this accommodation of religion when we come to consider wonder's relations with transcendence, and with ideas of the secular, in Chapter 9.

There is another aspect of Spinoza's treatment of religious narratives of prophecies and miracles which is central for the concerns of this book. He provided a model for the critique, not just of scriptural texts, but more broadly of the prevailing cultural 'narratives' or 'fictions' which shape the operations of social power. There are continuities here that connect his critique of Scripture with the vague but powerful image of the subversive gadfly through which Plato sketched the ideal of Socratic questioning.[4]

How do Spinoza's insights into the social power of religious narratives bear on his treatment of wonder? Insight into the operations of the dominant fictions of a culture can take thought in new directions. Through its connections with imagination, wonder plays a part in demystifying the theologians' exploitation of religious mysteries. That gives wonder a social role which goes beyond the part it plays as a stimulus to theoretical enquiry. Wonder, at the nexus of the interactions between reason, imagination and emotion, can initiate exposure of the operations — and obfuscations — of social power.

Faced with dogmatic theologians who maintained their power over the multitude by posing as authoritative interpreters of objective truth, Spinoza insisted that the familiar social narratives of his time should properly be understood as constructs of imagination. Those narratives, he thought, help shape a people's understanding of who they are and what they are about — of what matters in their past, and in their collectively imagined future. Yet he saw also that such stories, if they are misconstrued as definitive truths — if they stop people 'wondering enough' — can threaten the collective well-being they make possible.

Spurious certainties can debilitate the life of the mind. The familiar fictions that help bind a human collectivity together can also come to restrict the freedom of minds to move; they can become a source of intellectual paralysis. We acquiesce in that hardening of thought when we come to treat frequently repeated social narratives as objective truths. Wonder – as Spinoza understood it – is an expression of the mind's resistance to that insidious mental paralysis. We will see more of this aspect of wonder in Chapter 8.

The idea that wonder should be seen as a 'distraction' can seem like a trivialisation of the state that ancient Greek philosophers had credited with being the 'beginnings' of the profound intellectual activity associated with philosophy. Yet Spinoza's re-categorising of wonder had far-reaching ramifications in its subsequent history. In resisting its association with *passivity*, he drew wonder into the mind's *activity*. Although it introduces a pause into that activity, wonder is for him not the intrusion of something alien or threatening. It is integral to intellectual activity – an aspect of the striving for understanding which is the very essence of the mind's being. In that respect, Spinoza's version of wonder is closer to the ancient Greek accounts of wonder's role in intellectual enquiry than the Cartesian view of it as a passion could possibly be.

Spinoza derided Descartes' suggested remedy for the immobilising effects of the element of surprise in wonder, insisting that the mind can – of its nature – provide its own remedy. Yet he did share Descartes' concern that the mind should not be reduced to gaping stupor, to the detriment of intellectual inquiry. The idea that wonder was something that needed to be allayed in the pursuit of knowledge persisted into the eighteenth century. Adam Smith, in an early essay which was published posthumously, reflected on the place of philosophy among the sciences and the 'agreeable arts'. He commented there on the unsettling effects for intellectual inquiry of surprise at what is uncommon. Philosophy, he observed, seeks through finding regularities to soothe the mind, allaying the 'wandering in uncertainty' induced by surprise and wonder.[5]

Later developments in the history of wonder would come to see in Descartes' metaphor of immobilisation a more positive image of the disposition to wordless recognition of strangeness — a symbol of its enriching emotional intensity, rather than a deplorable frustration of intellect. Those developments lie on the other side of the emergence of a different understanding of wonder — as an intense emotion, associated with aesthetic experience rather than with intellect. In the next chapter we will see the emergence of this new version of wonder — centred on the feeling of the sublime. We will then see, in Chapter 4, how some of the doctrines that underlay Spinoza's own treatment of wonder were absorbed — not always fully understood - through German Idealist philosophy into the ideas and sensibility of Romanticism, to contribute to the allure of the sublime.

Notes

1 René Descartes, *The Passions of the Soul* [1649], in *The Philosophical Writings of Descartes*, Vol. 1, trans. John Cottingham, Robert Stoothoff and Dugald Murdoch (Cambridge: Cambridge University Press, 1985), Part. 1, Sec. 27, pp. 338–9. Further page references will be given in the main text.
2 Lorraine Daston and Katharine Park, *Wonders and the Order of Nature, 1150–1750* (New York: Zone Books, 2001), Chapter VII, 'Wonders of Art, Wonders of Nature', p. 260.
3 Benedict de Spinoza, *Ethics* [1677], in Edwin Curley, ed. and trans., *The Collected Works of Spinoza*, Vol. I (Princeton: Princeton University Press, 1985), Part III, Definition 3, p. 493. Further page references will be given in the main text.
4 These aspects of Spinoza's treatment of imagination are discussed more fully in my book (with Moira Gatens), *Collective Imaginings: Spinoza, Past and Present* (London and New York: Routledge, 1999).

5 Adam Smith, 'The Principles Which Lead and Direct Philosophical Inquiries, As Illustrated By The History of Astronomy', in his *Essays, Philosophical and Literary* [1795], ed. Joseph Black and James Hutton (Charleston: Nabu Press, 2010), p. 371.

3

Burke and Kant on the Sublime

For Descartes it was a 'primary' passion. For Spinoza it was not a passion at all, but rather a 'distraction' of the mind. Different though their attitudes were to wonder and its role in relation to knowledge and to human well-being, they both saw it as a state akin to awe. Wonder was for them a thought-stopping response to something strange and unfamiliar, which demands to be understood. For both, the concept of wonder was captured by the Latin term *admiratio*, with its connotations of something exceptional and impressive. Whether the surprise implicit in wonder unfolds as veneration or as dread, the object of wonder was seen as something out of the ordinary. This aspect of wonder – its direction to what is momentous, to what is potentially overwhelming – gave it strong associations with religion. It also underlies its close connections with the eighteenth-century fascination with the idea of *the sublime*.

Burke's Sublime: Horror and Delight

Edmund Burke's name is now most readily associated with his writings and speeches on political life. He is best known for his sceptical attitude towards the enthusiasm generated among his contemporaries by the spectacle of the French Revolution. His famous *Reflections on the Revolution in France* was published in 1790, some three decades after *A Philosophical Enquiry into the Origins of Our Ideas of the Sublime and Beautiful*, first published in 1757. In the intervening period, Burke wrote in response to other political events. *Thoughts on the Cause of the Present Discontents*, published in 1770, addressed issues of parliamentary representation and popular rights. Many of his parliamentary speeches were also circulated – including his famous oration in 1775, in defence of the American rebellion.

Those later writings on the practice of politics, and on the significance of particular political events, reflect Burke's more directly philosophical concerns in the *Enquiry*, namely, the nature of human passions, and their specific differences. He was interested, especially, in the interplay of the passions and imagination, and the ways in which those interactions are intensified – often independently of reason – by the operations of language. Although it is tempting to see Burke's *Enquiry* as a young man's foray into philosophy – left behind as he develops his mature involvement in the complex practicalities of political life – there is much in this early treatise that has continuities with his later preoccupations.

The *Enquiry* explores themes associated with custom, habit and convention; with the social roles of sympathy and imitation in intensifying emotion; with the social significance of manners and decorum; and with the role of words in shaping opinions and attitudes. For my purposes here, what is most important about Burke's treatment of the sublime is the reconfiguration it offers of wonder's relations with other emotions.

The idea of a difference between the sublime and the beautiful was a common topic of debate among Burke's contemporaries.

Their interest in it arose partly from the circulation in translation of an ancient Greek fragment, *On the Sublime*. The text was of uncertain origins, though commonly thought to date from the first century CE. Its authorship was attributed to Longinus, of whom little else is known. The subject matter of *On the Sublime* echoes Aristotle's concern in his *Poetics* with the nature of tragedy and the emotions associated with it; but the work has a strong emphasis on issues of literary style, rather than on the principles of dramatic composition.

Although the idea of the sublime belongs mainly in the philosophical subject area now identified as 'aesthetics', it was of broader significance in eighteenth-century debates. Through its bearing on the operations of collective imagination and emotion, it was relevant to issues of society and politics. It was also associated with religion, through its connections with ideas of transcendence. However, it figured especially in discussions on the objectivity of judgements made in critical evaluations of art and literature.

David Hume's essay, 'Of the Standard of Taste', was published shortly before the first edition of Burke's *Enquiry*. In it Hume argued for the recognition of objective standards in relation to the criticism of artistic performance and literary expression. Burke added to the second edition of his *Enquiry*, published in 1759, an 'Introduction on Taste' which expressed a similar concern that aesthetic judgements should not be treated as mere expressions of subjective preference or prejudice. For both Burke and Hume, reflection on 'taste' had wider implications for the understanding of judgement and of objectivity.

To make sense of later developments in the idea of the sublime, it is illuminating to first consider how Burke's analyses in the *Enquiry* relate to older versions of wonder. For a start, there is the striking fact that, in his discussion of particular passions, Burke does not mention wonder by name. If we want to locate it in his cartography of emotions, we find it split between 'curiosity' and 'astonishment'. Whereas for Descartes 'astonishment' was an excess of wonder, for Burke 'curiosity' and 'astonishment' are separated from one another by the associations of 'astonishment' with the exalted concept of the sublime. 'Curiosity', though it takes pride of place as the first emotion discussed in the *Enquiry*, is for him a tamer perturbation.

Echoing Descartes' account of wonder in the *Passions of the Soul*, Burke opens Part I of the *Enquiry* by declaring that 'the first and the simplest emotion which we discover in the human mind, is Curiosity'. He defines it as 'whatever desire we have for, or whatever pleasure we take in novelty'. As in the older accounts of wonder, curiosity is here treated as the condition which initiates intellectual inquiry. Yet, rather than seeing the restlessness it induces as indicative of profundity, Burke describes curiosity as the most superficial of all human affections – perpetually changing its object. It is, he says, an appetite which is 'very sharp but easily satisfied', and which 'has always an appearance of giddiness, restlessness and anxiety'.[1]

On Burke's analysis, curiosity lacks the strength and persistence necessary to make it of itself a significant emotion. It involves a trivial form of mental agitation – a mere ripple of surprise – in comparison with the state of astonishment produced by what is sublime. Curiosity, in its pure form, depends on novelty; and novelty quickly passes into familiarity. Yet, those connections with novelty ensure that curiosity 'blends itself more or less with all our passions'. For some degree of novelty must be 'one of the materials in every instrument which works upon the mind' (p. 27).

Hume, in his treatment of specific emotions in the *Treatise of Human Nature*, had also replaced wonder – in the form in which it stimulates the search for knowledge – with a passion he described as 'curiosity or the love of truth'. In the concluding section of Part II of the *Treatise*, he discusses that 'curious affection', which he credits with being the source of all his own inquiries. Hume's account of it emphasises the interactions of imagination and emotion. It also employs, as older accounts of wonder had done, metaphors of mental motion, which express the mind's delight in its own activity. Yet the tone of his talk of curiosity is very different from that of those earlier celebratory descriptions of wonder.

Hume's account of the pursuit of intellectual inquiry is deliberately playful. He ironically deflates the pretensions of philosophers to reach deeply into the natures of things. Famously, he here compares the motivational structure of philosophical thinking to the supposedly more light-hearted pleasures of hunting and gaming. The philosopher may need a justifying interest in the supposed social utility of his labours to get his mind into motion, but what really drives his inquiry is not that attending 'idea of utility', but rather the sheer pleasure of the chase.

In substituting curiosity for wonder, Hume does not reserve a more exalted place among the passions for any state resembling Burke's 'astonishment' at the sublime. He offers no evocations of transcendence, whether supernatural or secular. His playful treatment of curiosity reinforces his sceptical stance on grandiose ideals. The kind of philosophical life he sketches here lacks the magnificence of the 'greatness of soul' which had once been associated with the kind of thinking that begins in wonder. The Humean model of philosophical thought presents it as, above all, a sociable pursuit. It is pleasurable and agreeable, but it is not sublime.

Burke's version of 'curiosity' is similar to Hume's, though less playfully expressed. He defines it in terms of a propensity to novelty. The curiosity that initiates inquiry involves surprise, but it is not an analogue of the profound wonder that Plato and Aristotle cast in the role of the beginnings of philosophy. His treatment of 'astonishment', in contrast, has some strong continuities with older celebrations of wonder, but its associations are with aesthetic experience, rather than with scientific pursuits.

When Burke gets to discussing astonishment – in Part II of the *Enquiry* – he relates it closely to the experience of the sublime. It is caused by 'the great and sublime in *nature*, when those causes operate most powerfully'. Astonishment involves a pause in mental activity in the face of something unfamiliar; but Burke puts much more emphasis on the potential to inspire fear, rather than mere surprise: 'Astonishment is that state of the soul, in which all its motions are suspended, with some degree of horror.' He talks in this context of 'admiration' – the term whose Latin version *admiratio* was used by Descartes and Spinoza for the state known in English as 'wonder'. However, he explicitly relegates it to an inferior status to 'astonishment'. Along with 'reverence' and 'respect', admiration is a less horrifying effect of the sublime (Part I, Sec. I; p. 47).

Despite its strong associations with power and fear, Burke's sublime is supposed to produce in us a disconcerting mixture of pain and pleasure. Pleasure in the experience of the sublime depends, of course, on being at a safe distance from its dangerous power. Yet removal from great danger, he observes, leaves us 'impressed with a sense of awe, in a sort of tranquillity shadowed with horror' (Part I, Sec. III; p. 30). The sublime involves 'sympathetic', rather than 'direct' experience of horror. The conjunction of intense emotion with both sympathy and detachment gives Burke's sublime its aesthetic significance – its place in discussion of the critical evaluation of 'taste'.

Detachment may seem a strange companion to sympathy. Burke's point is that it is only at a distance that the communication of deep feeling can take place. It is through the conjunction of sympathy and detachment that poetry, painting and other 'affecting arts' are able to 'transfuse their passions from one breast to another, and are often capable of grafting a delight on wretchedness, misery, and death itself' (Part I, Sec. XIII; p. 38). The poet's efforts in bringing that about can be objectively evaluated, he insists, in accordance with 'standards of taste'.

Longinus had treated Homer's evocations of fear and danger as a prime illustration of the capacity to render the sublime in literary form. Echoing the Homeric examples, and filling them out with his own illustrations from Milton, Burke speaks of the sublime, with its power to excite ideas of terror, as 'productive of the strongest emotion which the mind is capable of feeling' (Part I, Sec. VII; pp. 33–4).

The experience of the sublime is supposed to be a confrontation with power, bordering on terror; yet it also produces in us an increased sense of our own worth. In Burke's summary of Longinus' account of this odd concatenation, it yields a sense of 'glorying' and of 'inward greatness', that 'always fills the readers of such passages in poets and orators as are sublime' (Part I, Sec. XVII; p. 43). In his own accompanying description of the phenomenon, the sublime

> produces a sort of swelling and triumph that is extremely grateful to the human mind; and this swelling is never more

perceived, nor operates with more force, than when without danger we are conversant with terrible objects, the mind always claiming to itself some part of the dignity and importance of the things which it contemplates.

In the experience of the sublime we are, it seems, not abject but exultant.

This intermingling of horror and delight in 'astonishment' is a new configuring of the elements of traditional wonder. The interruption of mental activity had been central to older accounts of wonder; but it was something to be remedied or accommodated by reason. On Burke's account, rather than demanding an intensifying of the activity of rational thinking, consternation serves to expose the inherent limitations of reason: 'The mind is so entirely filled with its object, that it cannot entertain any other, nor by consequence reason on that object which employs it. Hence arises the great power of the sublime, that far from being produced by them, it anticipates our reasonings, and hurries us on by an irresistible force' (Part II, Sec. 1; p. 47).

We have seen that for Descartes astonishment had a dangerous stupefying effect on the mind's power of reasoning – which could, however, be remedied by the exercise of rational will – whereas for Spinoza, the pause in thought brought its own restorative striving for understanding. For Burke, astonishment – the passion produced by the sublime – operates independently of reason. Rather than being ancillary to our efforts to think, it takes precedence over them.

What has happened in all this to the concept of wonder? Burke mentions the term only by way of warning against being too much taken up in questions of terminology. Several languages, he notes, frequently use the same word to signify indifferently the modes of astonishment or admiration and those of terror. Thus the same word *thamos* is in Greek either fear or wonder.

> The Romans used the verb *stupeo*, a term which strongly marks the state of an astonished mind, to express the effect either of simple fear, or of astonishment; the word *attonitus,* (thunderstruck) is equally expressive of the alliance of these ideas; and do not the French *etonnement* and the English *astonishment* and *amazement*, point out clearly the kindred emotions which attend fear and wonder? (Part II, Sec. II; p. 48)

Yet Burke's separation of 'curiosity' from 'astonishment' – across the conceptual chasm of the causal origins of astonishment in the sublime – makes the position of wonder in this cartography of the passions of much more consequence than the vagaries of terminology. The 'curiosity' that begins intellectual inquiry is now a world apart from the stupefying 'astonishment' that leaves reason behind under the impact of the power of the sublime.

In intellectual inquiry, clarity is a prerequisite of the pursuit of truth. The poetic expression of the sublime, in contrast, is intensified by obscurity and confusion; it abhors clarity. Thus Burke says of Milton's powerful description of Satan: 'The mind is hurried out of itself, by a croud of great and confused images; which affect because they are crouded and confused' (Part II, Sec. IV; p. 51). The power of the sublime to act on our feelings is independent of the degree of clarity of the images it evokes. 'In reality a great clearness helps but little towards affecting the passions, as it is in some sort an enemy to all enthusiasms whatsoever' (Part II, Sec. IV; p. 50). It is a double-edged remark. Burke's point was not to endorse enthusiasm; it was, rather, to insist that good sense demands that we acknowledge the strength of the passions and the power of rhetoric in shaping human action.

Again, the crucial point is the connection of the idea of the sublime with that of power. In representing it, the demands of clarity become an obstacle rather than a help. When we have traced power 'through its several gradations unto the highest of all', our imagination is 'finally lost'. Here there is no clarity or adequacy of representation to be had. Yet this power which lies beyond the limits of clear thought is 'undoubtedly a capital source of the sublime' (Part II, Sec. V; p. 58).

This 'capital' source of the sublime lies, it seems, beyond human capacities for adequate knowledge. The abandoning of 'clarity' and 'distinctness' – as Descartes called them – as the criteria of truth marks the distance of Burke's sublime from rationalist ideals of knowledge. It also indicates its intersections with ideas of transcendence inspired by religion. The relations between reason and the experience of the sublime become clearer in Burke's treatment of 'Words' in the final section of the *Enquiry*. Here too there are important implications for understanding what, in the reconfiguration of elements, has become of wonder.

In discussing language earlier, Burke stressed that sound, no less than sight, can be a source of the sublime. He addressed there something which will be a major concern in his later works on revolution and the power of crowds. It is, he says, not only the sounds of vast cataracts, raging storms, thunder or artillery that induce awe. The shouting of multitudes has a similar effect. By the sole strength of sound, the imagination is so amazed and confounded that 'in this staggering, and hurry of the mind, the best established tempers can scarcely forbear being borne down, and joining in the common cry, and common resolution of the croud' (Part II, Sec. XVIII; p. 68).

The central point is, again, that the sublime acts on us in ways that bypass reason. A crowd's shouting is a dramatic instance of a power that already resides in more everyday uses of speech. In the concluding sections of the *Enquiry*, Burke discusses more directly this affective power of words. The business of poetry and rhetoric, he says there, is not with succeeding in exact description; it is rather to affect an audience through sympathy: 'to display rather the effect of things on the mind of the speaker, or of others, than to present a clear idea of the things themselves' (Part V, Sec. V; pp. 136–7).

The suggestion that the art of rhetoric is concerned primarily with persuasion – with the power to convince, rather than with the discovery of truth – is hardly an original or controversial claim. However, Burke goes further. For him words have an affective power that operates differently from the model of the classical orator's power to convince. The connections of the notion of the sublime with sympathy are such that our passions are aroused much more through the circulation of 'opinions' than through rational understanding. 'Certain it is, that the influence of most things on our passions is not so much from the things themselves, as from our opinions concerning them; and these again depend very much on the opinions of other men, conveyable for the most part, by words only' (Part V, Sec. VII; pp. 137–8).

Words allow, as Burke puts it, 'the contagion of our passions'. We 'catch a fire already kindled in another, which probably might never have been struck out by the object described'. They allow for a strength of expression which is utterly different from clarity. Naked verbal description, no matter how exact, could scarcely have the smallest effect on us, were the speaker not able to call to his aid 'modes of speech that mark a strong and lively feeling in himself'. 'We yield to sympathy what we refuse to description' (Part V, Sec. VII, p. 139).

If the 'astonishment' produced by Burke's sublime is to be seen as a version of wonder, it is one which has largely lost its old connections with intellectual inquiry, rational deliberation and even the desire for clarity. What was profound in wonder seems here to be seen as having broken free of reason to enter the realm of horrified delight. Later, Immanuel Kant will reclaim the sublime for reason. Burke resisted the old idea of Longinus that sublimity manifested heroic grandeur or greatness of soul. The Kantian sublime will, in contrast, find expression in the idea of reverential awe directed precisely at the human capacity for reason.

Kant's Sublimity of the Mind

Kant's early essay, *Observations on the Feeling of the Beautiful and Sublime*, was published in 1764. As the title suggests, the distinction between the beautiful and the sublime is here primarily between different 'feelings'; but Kant extended it to cover a wide array of contrasts in human dispositions and temperaments, as well as to more transient states. 'Affability is beautiful, thoughtful silence sublime.'[2] It applies to the differences between national traits and tastes, as well as to the cultivation of individual character. Notoriously, he also aligned it with the differences between the sexes: 'The fair sex has just as much understanding as the male, but it is a *beautiful understanding*, whereas ours should be a *deep understanding*, an expression that signifies identity with the sublime' (p. 78). The distinction is also applied to literary genres: tragedy is distinguished from comedy chiefly in that it stirs the feeling for the sublime, rather than that for the beautiful.

The contrasts at times verge on the comical, and the general tone of the essay is lighter in tone than many of Kant's works. Yet there is a serious moral intent in his applications of the distinction. Although it has been taken mainly as a work on aesthetics, Kant's interest in the experience of the sublime reflected a growing concern with ideas of intellectual and moral character. In his own marginal comments on the work, he commented on the influence of Rousseau on his current aims. He makes it clear that his own intellectual commitments were challenged by Rousseau's critique, in his *Discourse on the Arts and Sciences*, of the presumption that humankind is benefited through supposed advances in knowledge. Kant talked in those marginal comments of his own consuming thirst for theoretical knowledge, and of his restless desire to advance it. Rousseau's critique had brought him, he says, to rethink his concern with the 'ends of reason'. He was coming to see that his treatment of reason should be expanded to take in practical, rather than just theoretical, goals – directly fostering the well-being of humanity, rather than merely encouraging idle speculation into the natures of things.[3]

Kant follows Longinus and Burke in stressing the intermingling of horror and delight in the sublime:

> The sight of a mountain whose snow-covered peak rises above the clouds, the description of a raging storm, or Milton's portrait of the infernal kingdom, arouse enjoyment but with horror; on the other hand, the sight of flower-strewn meadows, valleys with winding brooks and covered with grazing flocks, the description of Elysium, or Homer's portrayal of the girdle of Venus, also occasion a pleasant sensation but one that is joyous and smiling. (p. 47)

His version of the sublime, though superficially similar to Burke's, has a greater internal complexity. Not only does it apply to a range of different kinds of thing, it also comes in varying forms. In the early sections of the essay, he explains: 'Its feeling is sometimes accompanied with a certain dread, or melancholy; in some cases merely with quiet wonder; and in still others with a beauty completely pervading a sublime plan.' The first, he calls the 'terrifying' sublime; the second, the 'noble'; and the third, the 'splendid' (pp. 47–8). Wonder – as a state of fixity – figures in some of Kant's descriptions of the experience of the sublime, but it is not separated out as a feeling worthy of being described in its own right.

In Kant's fuller development of the concept in his *Critique of Judgement*, first published in 1790, the sublime replaces wonder as the feeling most closely associated with the mind's capacity to reason. In the section called 'Analytic of the Sublime', in Part I, Book II of that *Critique*, Kant presents the sublime as an 'indeterminate concept of reason'. The reference to 'indeterminacy' marks an important conceptual difference between Kant's sublime and beautiful. The beautiful appeals by virtue of its *form*. The sublime, in contrast, engages our attention through its *formlessness*. In a further distinction, the indeterminacy of the Kantian sublime comes in two kinds – the 'mathematically' and the 'dynamically' sublime. In both cases, the sublime stirs the mind to a realisation that there is within it a way of thinking which reflects the intellectual side of its nature, rousing it to an awareness of the supremacy of the ideas of reason over mere 'sensibility'.

In the case of the 'mathematically' sublime, that superiority is expressed in reason's capacity to grasp the idea of a totality, which imagination can present only one portion at a time. Kant illustrates the point by reference to travellers' apprehending the enormity of the Pyramids. To get the full emotional effect of the size of the monuments, the viewers must avoid coming too near, just as much as remaining too far away. Although that illustration of imagined measurement is, in an obvious sense, 'mathematical', Kant's point is a more general one. In the experience of the sublime, the imagination finds itself struggling in a fruitless effort to exceed its own limits. It is then forced to 'recoil upon itself', but in doing so, it 'succumbs to an emotional delight'.[4] The crucial point here is that the superior faculty of reason is elicited in us by the imagination's struggle to apprehend what lies ever beyond its capacities.

Kant's description of the struggling imagination echoes Burke's talk of the joyful 'swelling' and 'triumph' of the mind in the realisation of its own powers, as it strives to comprehend the sublime. However, Kant's version of that struggle is more explicitly a celebration of reason. He insists that the sublime resides not in objects but in thought — a cast of mind. 'True sublimity must be sought only in the mind of the judging Subject, and not in the Object of nature that occasions this attitude by the estimate formed of it' (p. 104).

In the case of the 'mathematically' sublime, the associated self-esteem remains comparatively cerebral — a pride in reason's capacity to form ideas which the imagination cannot encompass. In Kant's exposition of his second kind of sublime, the power of reason takes on a much greater emotional intensity. The 'dynamically sublime' has all the connotations of awe and terror that Burke had given it. Yet for Kant this sublime, too, is properly attributed, not to objects in Nature, but only to a way of thinking:

> Who would apply the term 'sublime' even to shapeless mountain masses towering one above the other in wild disorder, with their

pyramids of ice, or to the dark tempestuous ocean, or such like things? But in the contemplation of them, without any regard to their form, the mind abandons itself to the imagination and to a reason placed, though quite apart from any definite end, in conjunction therewith, and merely broadening its view, and it feels itself elevated in its own estimate of itself on finding all the might of imagination still unequal to its ideas. (pp. 104–5)

In the use that Burke made of the term – and in the common meaning which it now carries – many of us might indeed be inclined to see sublimity in the wild disorder of mountains or the dark, tempestuous ocean. Kant is deliberately restricting its application, while keeping its older associations with fear and the struggle for self-preservation, along with delight. He mentions with approval Burke's treatment of the sublime as 'a sort of delightful horror, a sort of tranquillity tinged with terror'. From Kant's perspective, however, Burke's description of the sublime remains 'merely empirical' – a 'physiological' account. He sees his own account as – in his special use of the term – a 'transcendental' exposition of aesthetic judgements: an account of the conditions under which those judgements are possible. 'The sublime must in every case have reference to our *way of thinking*, i.e. to maxims directed to giving the intellectual side of our nature and the ideas of reason supremacy over sensibility' (p. 127).

Kant wants to replace the supposed sublimity of 'wild' Nature with an exultation in human thought processes – and, more specifically, in the extraordinary capacities of human reason to transcend the limitations of imagination. Reason draws the imagination ever onward, yet continues to reach ever beyond it. Human reason itself here becomes something wondrous. Both the 'mathematical' and the 'dynamical' kinds of Kantian sublime bring a realisation of the power of reason. However, it is the dynamically sublime — associated with *might* and threat — that elicits the more striking articulation of the supremacy of human reason. To be able to relish that supremacy, we must of course be in a position of assured safety; but its basis is not a misguided conviction of our physical invulnerability. The bold overhanging rocks, the thunderclouds, the hurricanes, the boundless ocean make our power of physical resistance 'of trifling moment in comparison with their might'. Yet, provided we are secure, their fearfulness makes such things all the more attractive.

On Kant's analysis, what makes us want to call these things sublime is that 'they raise the forces of the soul above the height of vulgar commonplace, and discover within us a power of resistance of quite another kind, which gives us courage to be able to measure ourselves against the seeming omnipotence of nature' (pp. 110–11). Going further, he insists that sublimity therefore 'does not reside in any of the things of nature, but only in our own mind, in so far as we may become conscious of our superiority over nature within, and thus also over nature without us (as exerting influence upon us)' (p. 114). Nature's irresistible might forces on us a recognition of our physical helplessness, but it also reveals in us, in our humanity, a 'pre-eminence' of quite another kind. The mind comes to realise 'the appropriate sublimity of the sphere of its own being, even above nature' (pp. 111–12).

What is new in all this is not that the workings of the human mind are seen as an appropriate object of wonder. We have seen that already in the thought of Spinoza. What is novel in Kant's notion of the sublime is the suggestion that it is *only* the power of human reason that is really an appropriate object of wonder. The sublime is supposed to reside in the human mind — not because it is unreal, but because the sublime is indeed our way of thinking, at any rate when we are thinking at our best.

Clearly, not everything we might now think of as an object of wonder satisfies Kant's exalted criteria for the sublime – even in his secondary sense of something which elicits in us the exercise of our rational capacities. What is less clear is how exactly the Kantian sublime relates to older versions of wonder. Is it just a restriction on the application of an old concept? Or does it represent, rather, a major conceptual shift in the understanding of wonder itself?

Spinoza had insisted that wonder was a 'distraction' of the mind's activity rather than, as Descartes thought, a 'passion'. We are now in a position to better grasp why that difference in articulating the nature of the mind's temporary loss of activity was not a trivial one. Kant's treatment of the sublime does not respond directly to Spinoza. Yet it allows us to see more clearly what is at stake in denying wonder the status of a 'passion'. Kant's treatment of the state he calls the 'feeling of the sublime' relocates the description of wonder into a more nuanced account of the mind's activity. To fully grasp the conceptual shift involved here, we need to see Kant's treatment of the sublime in the context of all three Kantian *Critiques*, construed as a unified project. The crucial point about that unified project has been succinctly expressed by Gilles Deleuze in his commentary, *Kant's Critical Philosophy*.

Deleuze on the Struggle of the Faculties

For Deleuze, the interconnected argumentation of Kant's three *Critiques* amounts to 'an extraordinary undertaking'. He argues that, taken together, the works illuminate the tensions, and ultimate coordination, between different and rival faculties of the human mind, each of which has its own 'interests' – imagination, understanding and reason. In the first two *Critiques*, on this analysis, one dominant faculty exerts its rule over the others. In the *Critique of Pure Reason*, the dominance is exerted by *understanding*. Though it depends for its access to knowledge on what is delivered by imagination, understanding is also empowered to rein in the freedom of imagination. In the *Critique of Practical Reason*, the dominance lies with reason – in its 'practical', rather than its 'speculative' interest. Here, practical reason is able to form *ideas* of what lies beyond the reach of knowledge. Each faculty strives to reach beyond its own limits; yet there is, in their interaction, an intimation of a harmonising between them. That resolution, however, remains only an intimation until the third and final *Critique*. 'As regards a ground for the harmony of the faculties, the first two Critiques are completed only in the last.'[5]

On Deleuze's reading, it is that coming together of the faculties – each seeking its own limit – that is Kant's main concern in the *Critique of Judgement*. Each faculty pushes the other to its limit, while being forced to try to go beyond its own. This struggle between the faculties is central to Kant's treatment of the experience of the sublime. Here reason is involved in a terrible struggle with imagination. 'Imagination thus learns that it is reason which pushes it to the limits of its power, forcing it to admit that all its power is nothing in comparison to an Idea.'[6] The faculties confront one another, each stretched to its own limit, and find their accord in that fundamental discord.

Deleuze's reading is an interesting and, for our purposes, important interpretation of the intensity of the Kantian 'dynamical' sublime – of the volatile mix of emotions which it generates, and especially of its distinctive associations with power and struggle. Confronted with its own limits, the straining imagination experiences violence in its realisation that all its power is nothing in comparison with the Ideas of Reason. What is at stake here is not a simple relation of dominance and acknowledged subjection. It is an experience of conflict – in Deleuze's term, of *dissension*. Yet it is out of this violence that the 'accord' between the faculties emerges. The dynamical sublime is 'engendered' out of the conflict – not simply assumed in advance as a superiority. This paradoxical 'discordant accord' is for Deleuze the great discovery of the *Critique of Judgement*, making the work the foundation of Romanticism.

The eighteenth-century revival of the idea of the sublime complicates the story of wonder. It did not bring a contestation between rival accounts of its nature and role in knowledge – as in Spinoza's clash with the Cartesians. Rather, the focus shifted to an intense 'feeling of the sublime', disconnected from knowledge. The sublime became in some ways a surrogate for wonder. The Romantics – attracted to the affirmation of a condition seen as independent of Reason – had more affinity with Burke's sublime than with Kant's complex account of tensions and harmonising between faculties. However, as we will see when we return to Kant's 'Analytic of the Sublime' in Chapter 9, Kantian themes of struggle and yearning, directed towards something in principle unattainable, were also absorbed – with some significant adaptations – into the continuing allure of the Romantic sublime.

Notes

1 Edmund Burke, *A Philosophical Enquiry into the Origin of Our Ideas of the Sublime and Beautiful* [1757], ed. Paul Guyer (Oxford: Oxford University

Press, 2015), Part One, Section 1, p. 27. Further page references will be given in the main text.
2 Immanuel Kant, *Observations on the Feeling of the Beautiful and the Sublime* [1764], trans. John T. Goldthwait (Berkeley and Los Angeles: University of California Press, 1960), Sec. 2, p. 66. Further page references will be given in the main text.
3 The comment in Kant's marginalia is quoted and discussed by Frederick Beiser, in his essay 'Kant's Intellectual Development: 1746–1781', in Paul Guyer, ed., *The Cambridge Companion to Kant* (Cambridge: Cambridge University Press, 1992), pp. 43–4.
4 Immanuel Kant, *The Critique of Judgement* [1790], trans. James Creed Meredith (Oxford: Clarendon Press, 1952), pp. 99–100. Further page references will be given in the main text.
5 Gilles Deleuze, *Kant's Critical Philosophy*, trans. Hugh Tomlinson and Barbara Habberjam (Minneapolis: University of Minnesota Press, 1984), p. 24.
6 Deleuze, *Kant's Critical Philosophy*, p. 51.

4

Romanticism and the Allure of the Sublime

The Kantian sublime – with its connotations of a dynamic struggle between Reason and Imagination – did indeed, as Deleuze suggested, become a strong influence in the thought of the Romantics. So too did another version of mental struggle – Spinoza's idea of striving or *conatus* as the essence of the individual mind. Both those influences had significant consequences for the post-Kantian understanding of wonder.

The Sublime in Post-Kantian Idealism

The reception of Spinoza in the thought of the German Idealists – both in what was taken up of his thought and in what was ignored – is an important part of the story of what became of wonder in Romanticism. However, it is only when taken out of its own context that Spinoza's treatment of imagination can seem to lend support to Romantic repudiations of the supremacy of Reason. His doctrine of the world as the total expression of God under the attribute of matter – corresponding completely to that same God, equally expressed under the attribute of thought – resonated strongly for the Romantic Idealists, whatever their differences over what it might mean.

According to some, Spinoza treated God as disappearing into Nature. For others, on the contrary, Spinoza's philosophy contained too much God – a view famously held by Novalis, who described him as a 'God intoxicated man'.

More important, though, for understanding changing attitudes to wonder was the way Spinoza's concept of *conatus* or striving was appropriated. Against the background of Kant's emphasis on the struggle between Reason and Imagination, the striving for understanding took on intimations of a mood of endless, restless longing. Schelling, especially, admired the dynamic view of Nature that he found in what he took to be Spinoza's idea of *Natura Naturans*, which he construed as seeing the world as full of interconnected strivings, forming an actively self-developing whole.

Hegel, in his *Lectures on the History of Philosophy*, suggested that the German Idealists, including Fichte and Schelling, had recognised that 'the times called for life, for spirit'.[1] They had developed that idea to the point where Spirit came to be seen as both the forming power of Nature and the unfolding of intelligent comprehension. That anticipated in some ways, Hegel thought, his own notion of Spirit – the developmental model of Reason, which he offered, especially in the *Phenomenology of Spirit*, as a progressive hierarchy of states of human consciousness. The anticipations of Hegel were, in his own reckoning, particularly strong in the case of Schelling. He credited him – in contrast to Kant's 'meagre attempt at demonstrating spirit in nature' – with having recognised 'the ideal' as inhering in objective existence. Hence, he says, in Schelling's philosophy: 'Nature represents itself therein not as something alien to spirit, but as being in its general aspect a projection of spirit into an objective mode' (p. 535).

There is indeed an emphasis on active striving in Spinoza's concept of *conatus*; and there is also, in his treatment of mind and matter, a doctrine of parallel interconnected totalities. However, there is for him no possibility of finite modes of matter being transformed into finite modes of mind. His interconnected totalities fall a long way short of the dynamic forces of self-development Hegel found in Schelling. There is nothing in Spinoza's version of mind and matter as attributes of the one Substance that would lend support to the idea that there is no difference in kind, but only in degree, between the mental and the physical – both being seen as developments of the same forces. Nor did Hegel himself see Spinoza as the source of that view. However, he did - earlier in his Lectures – praise Spinoza's view of Substance as, in general, the foundation of all true views: 'Thought must begin by placing itself at the standpoint of Spinozism; to be a follower of Spinoza is the essential commencement of all Philosophy' (p. 257).

On the view Hegel attributed to Schelling, the totality of things - rather than consisting in parallel totalities of thought and matter – forms one huge unified structure. Within that unity, the more advanced forms of self-consciousness – typically expressed in philosophy and art – are nothing less than the highest development of the powers of Nature. The awareness of the world articulated in those higher forms of expression can then readily be seen as Nature developing through them its own fullness of self-awareness. It is a vision of mental and physical struggle which is consonant with the idea of the sublime. But it is not Spinoza. Nor is the mood of endless longing evoked in Romantic theory – the pervasive yearning for the unattainable – part of Spinoza's ideal of intellectual character.

Spinoza's concept of *conatus* was subject to the vagaries of later interpretation and appropriation; so too was Kant's account of the struggle between the faculties of the mind. We may conjecture what the future of wonder might have been, had it followed a firmer trajectory from Spinoza into post-Kantian thought. Spinoza's insights – especially into the status of wonder as a natural expression of the mind's inherent striving to understand the world and its own place within it – might have allowed wonder to keep more of its old connections with knowledge. The path of wonder might also have been different if Kant's treatment of the sublime had been seen – as he himself saw it – as belonging in a unified project, addressing the interactions of Imagination, Understanding and Reason. As it was, the repercussions of the sublime in Romanticism evoked a condition no longer closely connected with the celebration of intellect or reason – whether in Spinoza's or Kant's way of thinking of them.

In the writings of Schopenhauer, for example, the mind's inherent effort to understand took on connotations very different from Spinoza's emphasis on its joyful transitions to greater intellectual activity. Schopenhauer's version of the place of Reason in those efforts was also very different from Kant's depiction of its exhilarating struggle for 'discordant concord' with Imagination and Understanding. Schopenhauer regarded the cultivation of Reason as a form of pedantry. Those preoccupied with 'general maxims', he thought, almost always come off badly in life, showing themselves foolish, absurd and incompetent. The Will – a faculty which Spinoza refused to recognise – was for Schopenhauer superior to Reason; indeed, it was ultimately the only reality. He saw its endless dissatisfaction and disappointment as inherent in human life, which in consequence swings constantly between pain and boredom.

The Kantian experience of the sublime had been an awe-filled apprehension of grandeur, eliciting all that is best and highest in the human mind. In contrast to that confident celebration of the powers of human reason, Schopenhauer's vision of the outcome of the mind's ongoing efforts to know is accompanied by a deep sense of dread and disillusionment – a dismay, of cosmic proportions. He did, nonetheless, in an Appendix to *The World as Will and Representation*, praise Kant's treatment of the sublime in the *Critique of Judgement* as incomparably more successful than his treatment of the beautiful. He thought that the Kantian sublime pointed in some respects forward to his own response to the challenge of articulating the nature of mind's relations with the world.[2]

The idea of the sublime appealed to Schopenhauer, although he shared none of Kant's hopes for the ultimate emergence of concord out of discord. For him the distinctive pleasure of exaltation associated with the experience of the sublime was focused on a transcendence of self. It brought a felt recognition of the power to detach oneself from the pressure of one's own individual will, to be subsumed into a higher force. It appealed to Schopenhauer for another reason, too. It was important for him – and through him for Nietzsche – in helping to explain the mixed pleasure and horror characteristically expressed by tragedy as an art form. Tragedy, for Schopenhauer, is the highest degree of the feeling of the 'dynamically sublime'. The 'pleasure of exaltation' which he found in it is in some ways a reprise of Kant's contrast between the frailty of human bodies against the might of Nature and, on the other hand, the immeasurable power of human reason to reach in thought beyond those annihilating forces.

For Schopenhauer, individual human will is a frail phenomenon in the face of stupendous might. There is no celebratory self-satisfaction here in a capacity to transcend – in any sense – the power of Nature. It is not only as bodies that we are powerless against that might. The sense of exaltation in something sublime comes, not from confidence in the power of reason, but in the struggle to break free from the limitations of individual selfhood – into transcendent Will.

The fascinations of the sublime lingered in the thought of the Romantics, but the Kantian exultation in the 'discordant accord' between Reason and Imagination waned. It was as if Imagination was seen as having broken free from the Kantian model of a harmonised unity among the competing faculties of the mind. Reason ceased to be an object of either astonishment or admiration. Yet the emotional intensity of the idea of the sublime continued to inspire art and literature, and the theorising of their creative activity.

The old connections between knowledge and wonder – and with them the appeal of wonder as a topic worthy of serious philosophical interest – weakened under two forces coming from different directions. The increased preoccupation with rigorous methods of scientific inquiry relegated wonder back to the ambivalent position Descartes had assigned it – at best, as a stimulus to begin inquiry; at worst, as an impediment to its successful completion in certainty. The ancient connections between wonder and the hope for knowledge went missing. From the other direction, wonder was displaced from the realm of aesthetic judgement by the intensity of the related idea of the sublime. On the one hand, 'wonder' became a vague alternative term for 'curiosity' – a weak and wavering beginning of inquiry. On the other hand, it became a tame substitute for the sublime in aesthetic experience: a capacity for mere surprise – without shock, threat or terror.

The spirit of fevered exaltation associated with the sublime is far removed from the intellectual mood that came to characterise the advance of modern science. Its emotional intensity seems diametrically opposed to the insistence on painstaking, methodical processes of thought. At the same time, the excitement of old-fashioned wonder – oriented towards knowledge – cannot compete with the intoxication of the sublime as a medium of artistic vision and literary expression.

In later chapters we will see how recent philosophical treatments of wonder have tried to re-connect with some of those older unities of knowledge, emotion and imagination. We will return to look more closely at the complexities of Kant's 'Analytic of the Sublime', in relation to the bearing on wonder of contemporary religious themes of transcendence. But, first, a brief illustrative look at a literary treatment of the allure of the sublime. Its appeal – and also its hazards – are captured in Mary Shelley's popular Gothic novel *Frankenstein,* the first version of which was published in 1818 – the year before the publication of Schopenhauer's *The World as Will and Representation.*

Mary Shelley's *Frankenstein*

The daughter of the political theorist William Godwin and of Mary Wollstonecraft – the famous author of *Vindications* of *The Rights of Men* and of *The Rights of Woman* – Mary Shelley brought to the creation of her character, Frankenstein, a deep awareness of the ideals of Reason associated with the Enlightenment. She was also attuned to the literary culture of the Romantic movement, through the circle of friends who frequented the Godwin household, and especially through her relationship with the poet Percy Bysshe Shelley, with whom she had eloped in 1814. She had considerable knowledge of developments in the natural sciences in the early nineteenth century. Although *Frankenstein* is written in the popular genre of the horror story, it reflects a context of public interest in scientific experiments and, more generally, in controversy around the relations between science and religion.

Contemporary debates about theories of life and the status of the human soul – including heated exchanges around themes of 'vitalism' – found their way into the content of *Frankenstein*. Those issues have a stronger presence in the first edition. The significantly revised edition of 1831 reflects the concern of the author – by then widowed and supporting a son – with avoiding social and religious controversy.

Shelley's Frankenstein experiments with adding life to an assemblage of body parts gathered from dead humans. The narrative captures the revulsion elicited at the time by such practices as raiding cemeteries to provide specimens for anatomical dissection. However, the emotional intensity captured in the work is not confined to the dread or horror associated with the macabre. *Frankenstein* also captures the excitement generated by the intellectual debates of the time, dramatised here in an imagined extraordinary enterprise: to understand and control the forces governing the emergence and development of human life. The story distils those currents of adventurous inquiry and intense emotion into the disastrous consequences of a single grisly experiment.

The narrative is framed by an evocation of exuberant aspiration to 'discovery' of a more literal kind: the exhilaration generated by voyages – real or imagined – of geographical exploration. That familiar Romantic motif of the exalted pleasures of sublime struggle and endurance under harsh conditions is played out here in a perilous – and ultimately failed – voyage to the Arctic in search of the North-West passage. Walton – the writer of letters which structure the narrative – has led the unsuccessful expedition. Its desolate outcomes set the scene for his meeting with the unfortunate Frankenstein, who tells him the tale of the events which brought him to those icy lands, in pursuit of the monstrous being he has created in his own version of the *hubris* of discovery.

Walton's description of his own failed aspirations echoes the tones of the Kantian dynamical sublime. The splendid spectacles of the region, even in the midst of the desolation of failure, have the power to elevate the explorer's soul from earthly concerns: 'Such a man has a double existence: he may suffer misery, and be overwhelmed by disappointments; yet when he has retired into himself, he will be like a celestial spirit, that has a halo around him, within whose circle no grief or folly ventures.'[3]

Frankenstein's own tale is both horrifying and pitiful, suffused with grandeur and pathos. It is a story of a tragic conflict of mood and attitude between two versions of scientific knowledge. In his naive youth, we are told, Frankenstein had absorbed with delight the wild fancies of 'natural philosophy' inspired by mystical sources – by Cornelius Agrippa, Paracelsus and Albertus Magnus. His dreams were undisturbed by reality as he 'entered with greatest diligence into the search of the philosopher's stone and the elixir of life' (p. 23). That early excitement persisted in his imagination long after he had intellectually abandoned such dreams in favour of the more systematic approaches to which his later education exposed him. His fascination with the effects of steam and electricity – with modern experimentation into the nature of thunder and lightning – was overlaid on old visions of raising ghosts and devils.

Frankenstein's account of his intellectual development is a tale of disillusionment, followed by the rediscovery of an old enthusiasm, now projected onto the new scientific methods. Initially he saw his arduous studies in empirical science as requiring him to exchange 'chimeras of boundless grandeur' for 'realities of little worth' (p. 30). However his eagerness for inquiry returns when he finds his admired professor of chemistry able to communicate a vision of comparable intensity to the one he had been forced to abandon. In a panegyric on the superiority of modern science, his mentor tells him that the modern masters, although they make no claims to transmute metals or find the elixir of life, have indeed 'performed miracles':

> They penetrate into the recesses of nature, and shew how she works in her hiding places. They ascend into the heavens; they have discovered how the blood circulates, and the nature of the air we breathe. They have acquired new and almost unlimited powers; they can communicate the thunders of heaven, mimic the earthquake, and even mock the invisible world with its own shadows. (pp. 30–1)

His professor describes the achievements of modern science in the language of the sublime; and Frankenstein is mesmerised by the vision that opens up. His vision of his own future in scientific discovery now has an emotional charge comparable to the explorer's talk of haloed celestial spirits. His feelings bear him onwards 'like a hurricane'. 'Life and death appeared to me ideal bounds, which I should first break through, and pour a torrent of light into our dark world' (p. 36).

In narrating the momentum of Frankenstein's rise and fall, Shelley's prose powerfully juxtaposes exhilaration and dread. Enthusiasm drives the scientist on through the collection of bones from the charnel houses – disturbing 'with profane fingers' the tremendous secrets of the human frame. Then, at the very moment of success, triumph turns to horror. Frankenstein flees as the yellow-skinned creature comes to life.

One of the striking achievements of Shelley's writing in this work is the way in which the horror of Frankenstein's situation is balanced with her sympathetic rendering of the situation of the creature. Frankenstein is brought close to madness as he contemplates the potential disasters he has unleashed on the unsuspecting world, to which he had hoped to bring unprecedented benefits. In counterpoint to that crushing disappointment, the reader is offered the creature's recounting of his own struggle to live in a world in which his monstrous appearance renders him frightening and alien.

The creature's account of his life draws amusingly – and often touchingly – on familiar literary and philosophical sources. Many readers of *Frankenstein* would have recognised in the story elements of Rousseau's narrative of the development of the human species, in his *Discourse on the Origins of Inequality*. Some would also have seen the creature's poignant demand that Frankenstein provide him with a female companion of his own kind in the light of Mary Wollstonecraft's sardonic critique, in her *Vindication of the Rights of Woman*, of Rousseau's treatment in *Emile* of the supposed complementarity of the sexes. The creature reports on his own reading – after impressively becoming literate, largely from his own resources: while walking in the woods he stumbled on a satchel containing *Paradise Lost*, a volume of Plutarch's *Lives*, and Goethe's *Sorrows of Werther*.

Frankenstein's nameless creature discovers knowledge – with some enjoyment – only to learn that it brings also heightened sorrow. In his later encounter with his maker, he tells him of his anguish at not having remained for ever in a native state, devoid of reflection beyond immediate sensation: 'Of what a strange nature is knowledge! It clings to the mind, when it has once seized on it, like a lichen on the rock' (p. 96). Self-education has brought the creature the torment of self-reflection. He contrasts his own condition with that of Adam – God's creature, as described by Milton – who came forth as a perfect creature, allowed to happily converse and learn from others, rather than being left 'wretched, helpless and alone' (p. 105).

The idea of the sublime is a constant presence throughout this story – in the form of landscapes of awesome beauty, which carry, nonetheless, intimations of dread. The 'sublime and magnificent' scenes which surround Frankenstein elevate him 'from all littleness of feeling', subduing and tranquillising his grief. His intense emotions respond to the sublime differently at different stages. He remembers a glacier which, before the disastrous experiment, had filled him with 'a sublime ecstasy', giving his soul wings which allow it to 'soar from the obscure world to light and joy'. The same scene is later experienced as a source of dread. Its 'solitary grandeur', which had previously elicited delight, is now shattered by the looming presence of his creature – bounding over crevices to confront him.

The setting for Frankenstein's final meeting with the creature, in the Arctic, is even more terrifying in its sublimity. The glaciers and ridges of inaccessible precipices have become the creature's fitting habitat. Frankenstein's visions of glory persist to the end, as he urges the sailors on Walton's doomed expedition to take pride in their readiness to encounter dangers, and even death, for the benefit of mankind. His own aspirations have played out in a disastrous outcome. Yet for him too something of the vision of the sublime remains intact. 'Seek happiness in tranquillity', he counsels Walton, 'and avoid ambition, even if it be only the apparently innocent one of distinguishing yourself in science and discoveries. Yet, why do I say this? I have myself been blasted in these hopes, yet another may succeed' (p. 186).

We are left to wonder where this leaves the idea of the sublime. The final irony of the story is that it is the pathetic creature who lays the final claim to sublimity. Filled with self-loathing, he declares his intention to complete the destructive course of his unfortunate life in an act of self-immolation, which has its own pretensions to grandeur. He tells Walton that he will seek the northern-most extremity of the globe, where he will assemble his funeral pyre. He will reduce to ashes his miserable frame, so that his remains may 'afford no light to any curious and unhallowed wretch' (p. 190) who might create such another as he has been. It is as much an anguished condemnation of his creator as it is an expression of remorse. The language of the creature's final speech poignantly evokes a thwarted capacity for gentle enjoyment, no less than a potentiality to wreak destruction:

> Light, feeling, and sense, will pass away; and in this condition must I find my happiness. Some years ago, when the images which this world affords first opened upon me, when I felt the cheering warmth of summer, and heard the rustling of the leaves and the chirping of the birds, and these were all to me, I should have wept to die; now it is my only consolation. (p. 190)

Creator and created both perish in the ruins of the scientist's glorious hopes. Yet the aspiration to the sublime retains its allure in the creature's defiant spirit. He taunts the dead Frankenstein: 'Blasted as thou wert, my agony was still superior to thine . . . I shall ascend my funeral pyre triumphantly, and exult in the agony of the torturing flames' (p. 191). The nameless, monstrous product of human ingenuity has the last word – and that last word is an exultant affirmation of the sublime.

There are unresolved tensions in the attitudes towards the sublime that are given such dramatic expression in *Frankenstein*. The ambivalence is perhaps deliberate. Certainly, it is artistically effective. The authorial stance is less ambiguous in the edition published in 1831; Frankenstein's scientific aspirations become less threatening to conventional orthodoxies. It is a shift of emphasis, rather than a significant change of content; yet the changes are revealing. In the first version, the horror resides partly within the depiction of the scientific endeavour; it is the dark side of the drive to know, rather than just the consequence of Frankenstein's disastrous individual flaws and mistakes. In the later version, the terrible outcomes are more clearly attributed to the failure to observe the restraints of judicious reasoning. Frankenstein has fallen under the influence of irreligious attitudes, fuelled by an overactive imagination.

In the Introduction to the later edition Mary Shelley emphasised the religious aspects of Frankenstein's dismay when he first gazes on the fruits of his labour: 'Frightful must it be; for supremely frightful would be the effect of any human endeavour to mock the stupendous mechanism of the Creator of the world. His success would terrify the artist; he would rush away from his odious handywork, horror-stricken.'[4] The difference in emphasis redirects the horror. Rather than arising from tensions within the drive to know, it now arises from a more explicit conflict between Frankenstein's desires and conventional expectations of piety. His fate is now primarily due to the bad influence of mistaken, irreligious, attitudes to knowledge.

In the 1818 version, there is a continuum in the young Frankenstein's passion for knowledge. The sense of wonder which is evoked in him by the old Renaissance works is at first dissipated by his education in modern scientific methods; then it is revived in a new form. The original emotional intensity with which he had devoured the old mystical texts returns as he enters more deeply into the 'miracles' of modern science. In the 1831 edition, there is a sharper distinction between the two stages. The element of magic – of the daemonic – in the desire for knowledge is now more firmly relegated to the past. Frankenstein's personal excesses of emotion and imagination become emblematic of the historical past of scientific inquiry. The disastrous outcomes arise from his misuse of knowledge – in defiance of the restraints of religious sensibility – rather than from dangers inherent in the very nature of intellectual inquiry.

Frankenstein is too good a novel for its insights to be encapsulated into simple messages. It reflects the controversies of its time about the relations between science – and the desire for knowledge, more broadly – and religion. It was, after all, written as a modern retelling of the legend of the punishment of Prometheus for his hubris in stealing the element of fire from Zeus, for the benefit of humanity. For my purposes here, what is striking about the novel is that it can be read as, among other things, a literary exploration of the notion of the sublime – its attractions; its dangers; its intensifying effects on the interactions of imagination and emotion.

The Romantic sublime came out of wonder, and its seductive power came to eclipse wonder's connections with the effort to know. It was as if it drew to itself the emotional intensity and adventurous imagining that had once given vitality to the operations of intellect. Both wonder and intellect suffered in the separation.

The Demise of the Sublime?

The sublime – especially in what Kant called its 'dynamical' form – continued to have significance for moral and religious consciousness. It has a strong presence in Kierkegaard's imaginative retelling of the story of Abraham and Isaac in his *Fear and Trembling*, published in 1843. Kierkegaard there has his narrator present Abraham as struggling to reconcile total obedience to divine command with his limitless love of – and sense of responsibility towards – his son. The story is told as depicting a crisis – a conflict between incompatible duties, which cannot be resolved through reason. Abraham's 'fear and trembling' can find no resolution in the acceptance of the rational order of things. His obedience to God's command is a leap of faith into the abyss; it reaches beyond all conventional understanding of an ethical demand.

In his embrace of conflicting demands, Kierkegaard's Abraham can be read as modelling a consciousness shaped to the idea of the sublime. His heroically willed sacrifice of Isaac is an enactment of *sublimity*. It is a cast of mind which can fit uneasily with the orientations of contemporary readers. Can we now accommodate the idea of the sublime as a model for intellectual or moral character? Sylviane Agacinski has offered a reading of Kierkegaard's Abraham story which argues persuasively that what we find strange in it shows the impossibility of appropriating the feeling of the sublime to contemporary consciousness. It involves, she argues, an exaltation of greatness, immensity, the absolute – along with formlessness and facelessness – all of which is alien to the modern acceptance of finitude.

Agacinski's reading of the text captures the mood of endless yearning for infinity which was part of the heritage of the

Kantian sublime in Romantic thought. Kant, as we have seen, located the sublime in the capacities of the human mind, so that it became the feeling of a supersensible faculty within us. Agacinski suggests that this interiorising of the sublime amounted in effect to an attempt to exorcise fear. It was as if we no longer needed to bow down before anything external, but only before the moral law within; nothing could be truly sublime except the voice of reason.

On Agacinski's analysis of what came later, Hegel's aesthetics retained the Kantian idea of the sublime as an attempt to represent the unrepresentable; but the idea of it as associated with moral law was abandoned. Hegel's philosophy thus implied the end of the sublime in both its religious and its moral forms. It remained only as an aesthetic category: 'If Abraham's sacrifice, or his devotion, can be described as aesthetically sublime, then they are no more than the transcended shapes of a transcended form of religious thinking.'[5] In effect, the sublime becomes 'mere poetry'; the idea of it as something we could really 'tremble' before has become alien to modern consciousness. Agacinski concludes that the Abraham of *Fear and Trembling* remains a stranger to us.

It may be a contentious reading of Kierkegaard. Yet it does capture something of the strangeness, now, of the sublime as a character ideal. Such a role was not advocated in eighteenth-century debates on the sublime. Burke was not interested in giving it moral significance. The sublime was not for him – as it had been for Longinus – a response to elevating thoughts. Hume also expressed reservations about the celebration of associated ancient ideas of greatness of soul, about which we will see more in a later chapter.

Agacinski's central point is that we can no longer see *ourselves* as sublime; that, in a mentality which accepts finitude, the sublime ceases to be something to which we can seriously aspire. What bearing does this have on the relations between wonder and the sublime? She is talking about Kierkegaard's Abraham as an ethical model, rather than about the sublime as it figures in accounts of aesthetic judgement – or of judgement more generally. Nor is she directly discussing Kant's argumentation about the sublime. Her concern is, rather, with the upshot of the idea of the sublime as we received it through Romanticism – its inappropriateness for our sense of ourselves under conditions of modernity. What bearing do her conclusions have on the relations between the sublime and the broader understanding of wonder?

One of the challenges in tracking the history of philosophical accounts of wonder is that the concept itself splits in ways that do not always correspond to conceptual changes. In the famous moving passages that conclude his *Critique of Practical Reason*, Kant talks of two things that fill his mind – and, by implication, the minds of his contemporaries – with ever new and increasing admiration and awe, the more he reflects on them: the starry heavens above, and the moral law within. If Agacinski is right, we can no longer take seriously the idea of awe or admiration at the moral law within us. Does that have any bearing on what has become of wonder at the starry heavens above?

We will return to these questions in Chapter 9, with a closer examination of the feeling of the sublime in relation to ideas of transcendence. First, let us track further the demise of the Romantic sublime – enacted through some of the literary works and theoretical reflections of one of its nineteenth-century critics, Gustave Flaubert.

Notes

1. G. W. F. Hegel, *Lectures on the History of Philosophy* [1840], trans. E. S. Haldane and Frances H. Simson (London: Routledge and Kegan Paul, 1974), Vol. III, p. 505. Further page references will be given in the main text.
2. Arthur Schopenhauer, *The World as Will and Representation* [1819], trans. and ed. Judith Norman, Alistair Welchman and Christopher Janaway (Cambridge: Cambridge University Press, 2010); Appendix: 'Critique of the Kantian Philosophy', pp. 441–566.
3. Mary Shelley, *Frankenstein or The Modern Prometheus: The 1818 Text*, ed. Marilyn Butler (Oxford: Oxford University Press, 1969), p. 16. Further page references will be given in the main text.
4. Included as an Appendix to the OUP edition of the 1818 text, p. 196.
5. Sylviane Agacinski, 'We Are Not Sublime', in Jonathan Rée and Jane Chamberlain, eds, *Kierkegaard: A Critical Reader* (Oxford: Blackwell, 1998), p. 139.

5

Wonder and Stupidity: Flaubert on Romanticism

Reflecting on his literary works in correspondence, Flaubert often talked of a state that he struggled to express in his writings – a way of apprehending things as simply *there*. He mentions it, in a letter of 1847 to his lover, Louise Colet, as an admirable achievement of Voltaire's in the final passages of *Candide*. The characters – after all the vicissitudes they have endured in their journeying through 'the best of all possible worlds' – are left to 'cultivate their garden'. Flaubert speaks of that calm, tranquil conclusion as the proof of Voltaire's genius: explicitly rejecting reflection on the final state of affairs, it asserts its own reality, and stops there, 'stupid like life itself'.[1] What impressed Flaubert was Voltaire's resistance to the definitive summing up of 'finalities'. He was shocked that Colet could have suggested that perhaps there was in fact no finality in that wonderful ending. 'What an extraordinary idea of yours', he wrote, 'that someone should continue *Candide*! Is it possible? Who will do it, who *could* do it? There are some works so overpoweringly great (and *Candide* is one of them), that their weight would crush anyone who tried to take them on.'[2]

Defining Stupidity

It is a striking observation on the ending of *Candide*. But what is it that connects this repudiation of 'finality' with stupidity of any kind – much less the supposed stupidity of life itself? In a passing remark in another letter, Flaubert elaborates on his aspiration to an unembellished form of writing. He would like, he says, to present things as if 'from the point of view of a *cosmic joke* – that is to say, as God sees them from on high'.[3] Again, it is a puzzling aspiration; and the connections between the expressions of the artistic ideal are elusive. A God's-eye view is more easily associated with omniscience than with stupidity. Yet there is a deep insight in these luminous, though perplexing, remarks. What is important for Flaubert about the divine perspective is not its objectivity but the detachment that makes possible the ironic 'cosmic joke'.

The 'stupidity' that fascinates Flaubert is not a deprivation of intelligence. Nor does he regard it as simple ignorance. He sees it, rather, as a condition which is inherent in human thought processes. Stupidity of this kind is not a specific flaw or deficiency in individual human beings; nor is it an aberrant feature of a particular society at a particular time. It is an ubiquitous feature of human thinking – a universal condition. In both its positive and its negative aspects, this apprehension of things as *just there* echoes themes we have seen in the philosophical history of wonder. Those resonances may help explain Flaubert's ambivalent attitudes towards stupidity – his need to expose it to ridicule at the same time that he seems strangely attracted to it.

In its resistance to finality – to being summed up – this form of stupidity has something in common with the mental stillness that ancient philosophers associated with wonder. Flaubert was drawn to a vision of Art and its relations with Truth which had affinities with those old concepts of wonder. Yet his treatment of stupidity also reverberates with more negative overtones. In an early letter to his friend, Louis Bouilhet, he offered a derisive definition of stupidity as 'wanting to reach a conclusion'. 'What mind worthy of the name, beginning with Homer, ever reached a conclusion?', he asked.[4] The form of stupidity he evokes there is a denial of thinking – a desire to round it off into something definite, which can be recited as an established truth. It could be seen as a refusal of the ongoing state that Plato had Socrates celebrate as sustained 'not-knowing'.

Flaubert's trenchant – though also perplexing – definition of stupidity as wanting to reach conclusions was suggested in the context of a discussion about his plan to write a *Dictionary of Accepted Ideas*, which was to be appended to his final work – the unfinished *Bouvard and Pecuchet*. However, his earlier works too are rich in enactments of the tensions and ambivalences within – and between – wonder and stupidity. It is no coincidence that, both in his novels and in his reflections on art and literature, he also expressed frustration with the sentiments and aspirations of Romanticism. He is not a theorist of the sublime; yet throughout much of his writing there is a vision of ways of apprehending the world which retain the intensity of wonder, without the orientation towards transcendence which was the mark of the Romantic sublime.

Wonder After the Sublime: Scenes from *Madame Bovary*

Madame Bovary, first published as a book in 1857, is in many ways an expression of Flaubert's own ambivalent attachment to

Romanticism, as well as of his efforts to develop literary strategies appropriate to his own artistic vision. Emma Bovary is a poignant embodiment of Romantic sensibility. She sees the world through the lens of the Romantic novels she has read in her youth. Her perceptions of what surrounds her – of her husband, her lovers and her social environment – are mediated through that mentality. It is also reflected in her propensity to interpret her own emotions through an exalted vision.

In the early stages of infatuation with her lover Rodolphe, Emma exults in her perception of herself as a loved woman: 'She was entering into something wondrous where all would be passion, ecstasy, delirium; a bluish immensity surrounded her; emotion's peaks glistened beneath her thought, and ordinary existence appeared only in the distance, far below, in the shade, between the intervals of these heights.'[5] Emma's predilection to Romantic posturing limits her sense of what is possible for her. When she eventually sees through the illusions she has projected onto her human lovers, she swings into an equally vehement religious sentimentality, reconstructing herself as a privileged ascetic recipient of a superior divine love.

Flaubert's descriptions of Emma's shifting states of mind unsettle the familiar iconography and clichés of Romanticism. There is, for example, a disturbing displacement of the familiar motif of love-evoked-by-moonlight in one of her scenes with Rodolphe:

> [The moon] climbed swiftly behind the poplars' branches that hid her here and there, like a black curtain full of holes. Then she appeared, blazing with whiteness, in the empty sky she had illuminated; and so, slowing on her course, she let fall upon the river a great stain, that made an infinity of stars; and this silvery glimmering seemed to writhe there, down to the depths, as if

it were a headless snake covered in luminous scales. And it was not unlike some monstrous candelabra too, from whose length streamed drops of melting diamonds. (p. 188)

When Rodolphe cries 'Ah, beautiful night!', his cry is mocked by the mixture of the wondrous and the sinister in the previous imagery of reflected moonlight. The scene carries an ironic barb at the expense of Romantic clichés. However there is also something else going on, which bears on ideas of artistic vision and truth. There is no authorial affirmation of the moonlight – either as benign, orderly beauty or as malevolent wildness. It is left unclear whether Rodolphe's cry expresses insistent naivety or sarcasm.

In thus mischievously juxtaposing cliché-ridden perceptions of moonlight with unnerving imagery of headless snakes and monstrous candelabra, Flaubert is not replacing one set of images by another that can be perceived as more objective. The shifts in imagery bring a powerful and disturbing alternative perspective, which has no more – but also no less – claim to truth. The startling redescription of the reflected moon shakes the familiar Romantic connotations of moonlight. Once upset, of course, those accustomed associations can appear stupid. Yet there is an ironic tone in the alternative description which intimates that – repeated often enough and with the right framing – the bizarre headless snake could also take on the lineaments of trite cliché.

There is in this exercise in redescription a kind of detachment which is enacted repeatedly throughout Flaubert's novels, and discussed in his correspondence. The authorial presence is broken into a multiplicity, in which no one voice or perspective is privileged. Flaubert talked in letters of the desirability of writing in such a way that readers would find in a book crowds of humans, into which the authorial voice would be broadcast, rather than expressing a single declamatory persona. It is a significant point, since crowds have an important place in Flaubert's novels. In many of his descriptions of them, what is offered is not a single viewpoint on a multiplicity, but a splitting of authorial perspective itself into a multiplicity.

The strategy is particularly striking in the famous description in *Madame Bovary* of a crowd gathered to listen to speeches at an agricultural show, where the narration shifts without warning between different verbal exchanges – presented, as if overheard, in direct speech, as well as in apparent comments from unidentified observers. A conversation between Emma and Rodolphe – appropriately about Romantic love – is positioned on a balcony above the crowd, to which they have withdrawn, as Rodolphe would have it, 'to enjoy the show more comfortably'. Their exchange is interspersed with the hollow pomposities of the speeches below them, the mundane aspirations of the 'menials' assembled to receive awards, and the noise of rough animal tongues tearing at foliage dangling from muzzles – in a telling implicit commentary on the quality of the municipal rhetoric.

The perspectival shifts throughout the narrative capture the social position of the characters, and the intersections of their preoccupations, as much as does the content of their thoughts. The couple's spatial positioning accentuates the contrasts between their exalted conversation and the more earthy sensibility enacted below them, allowing Rodolphe to better exploit Emma's Romantic propensities. There are in fact two moralities, he assures her:

> the petty, the expedient, the morality that belongs to man, that never ceases to change and bawls at the top of its voice, bustling

down below, workaday, like that gathering of imbeciles that you see there. But the other, the eternal one, lies all around and overhead, like the landscape that surrounds us and the open sky that gives us light. (p. 137)

Flaubert often uses narrative strategies to deny the possibility of an encompassing perspective, from which order and sense might be bestowed on what is happening. This distinctive authorial detachment is at its starkest in the scene of Emma's death, where there is no authorial stance enacting a prevailing order from which the reader is permitted to apprehend the event. The narration is numbing – both in form and in content. 'A convulsion knocked her back onto the mattress. Everyone drew nearer. She no longer existed.' As the next chapter begins, the narrator's voice moves swiftly from the particular to the general: 'There is always, after someone's death, a kind of stupefaction given off, so hard is it to take in this abrupt coming of nothingness and to resign oneself to believing it.' Then we are abruptly taken back to the personal particularity of Charles Bovary's wild 'Goodbye! Goodbye!' (pp. 311–12).

The details of the moment are graphic, yet there is about it all a strange – though truthful – lack of presence. We are offered a succession – or at any rate a juxtaposition - of viewpoints. Some are agonisingly close, others more distant, some almost comically distracting in their focus on the observers' own comparatively trivial interests and agendas. The multiple perspectives continue in the narration of the funeral procession, reviving earlier imagery of rustic exuberance – of fresh breezes and verdant crops, of dewdrops trembling beside paths and on thorn hedges: 'All kinds of joyous sounds filled the horizon; the banging of a cart rolling at a distance over the ruts, the cockerel's crow repeating itself or the scamper of a hen that you could see fleeing under the apple-trees' (p. 322). In the aftermath of death, multiple memories and impressions jostle in the strange coexistence of presence and absence which is the stuff of grief.

Flaubert's cleverly crafted shifts in perspective demand the reader's participation in moving between angles of vision. In the lack of an overriding authorial voice, the different viewpoints – and the emotions associated with them – coexist without resolution. In these literary strategies, there are insights at play into issues of truth, objectivity and detachment. There is no reassuring summation. Flaubert's vision is not optimistic, but nor is it insistently bleak. Reality here is arid only in the minds of those who become disillusioned, after previously seeing it as suffused with intelligible meaning or purpose.

Flaubert's own observations about his narrative strategies often seem to suggest a God-like vision. Yet what is at stake here is very different from ideas of an 'omniscient narrator' – even one who refrains from expressing his own opinions. Nor is it like the 'view from nowhere' invoked in twentieth-century philosophical discussions of objectivity, where the limitations of perspective are imagined as disappearing altogether.

When Flaubert talks in his correspondence of transcribing things as God sees them from on high, he is not expressing a Romantic Idealist yearning for access to a view of the whole. He is talking, rather, of an artistic vision which strives to apprehend the world free of imposed 'conclusions' – as 'just there'. His idealised artistic vision is more akin to Spinoza's detachment – of which we will see more later – than it is to the Romantic Idealist sense of the sublime as a yearning glimpse of transcendence.

'There are no more artists, as they once existed', Flaubert complained, in a letter to Louise Colet – 'artists whose loves and minds were the blind instruments of the appetite for the beautiful', who 'looked at human life with wonder, as we contemplate anthills'.[6] In another formulation of the point in a different letter to Colet, he says that an author in his book must be like God in the universe, present everywhere and visible nowhere. 'Art being a second Nature', he goes on, 'the creator of that Nature must behave similarly. In all its atoms, in all its aspects, let there be sensed a hidden infinite impassivity. The effect for the spectator must be a kind of amazement. "How is all that done?", one must ask; and one must feel overwhelmed without knowing why.'[7]

Flaubert's remarks on artistic vision are not polished enunciations of a theoretical position. They are the disjointed observations of a writer reflecting on his own writing practice – and on the mental condition he hopes to induce in his readers. Yet they offer broader glimpses into a post-Romantic vision of a form of wonder freed of the heady aspirations of the sublime. They evoke artistic striving, but the effort is directed to attaining a state of awed contemplation of what is already *there* – not to some transcendent goal or purpose in an unreachable beyond.

Let us now see how these insights play out in Flaubert's depiction of stupidity in the pursuit of knowledge, in *Bouvard and Pecuchet*.

Bouvard and Pecuchet

Flaubert's final work is a story of two clerks who are enabled, by an unexpected inheritance, to devote their lives to the pursuit of knowledge. Taken together, the projected novel and the *Dictionary of Accepted Ideas* provide some clues as to what made

Flaubert associate the desire to 'reach conclusions' with a kind of stupidity. They also help clarify the bearing of stupidity, thus understood, on wonder.

Stupidity, in the form in which Flaubert considers it here, seems at first sight the antithesis of the capacity for wonder. Yet their connections are not as simple as a direct opposition. There are nuances, as well as ambivalence, in Flaubert's attitude towards his characters' search for knowledge. *Bouvard and Pecuchet* is about wonder, no less than it is about stupidity. It addresses the conditions under which wonder can turn to stupidity, and the conditions under which such stupidity flourishes. It is also about ways in which the desire to know can itself become an impediment to wisdom. It allows us to see some of the ways in which we can be blinded by stupidity, and also ways in which it can be a collective rather than an individual condition.

Flaubert's doomed clerks are all too prone to wonder of the kind which drives the acquisition of knowledge. Their efforts to master vast areas of learning repeatedly come to grief. Yet, out of their passion to know – out of the sadness of their unsatisfied longings – there comes, for the reader, insight into the possibility of a genuine and sustainable wonder, which constantly eludes these characters.

Flaubert himself insisted that *Bouvard and Pecuchet* was a comic novel. It can indeed be read as a satire on the pursuit of knowledge. Finally, however, it is not the clerks that are the main object of its barbs. For all their flaws and foibles, there is poignancy in the description of their aspirations and their yearnings, and pathos in their failures. The two devoted friends are in the end seen as neither completely wise nor completely foolish. Ultimately, it is the collective stupidity of their social context that is made to appear ridiculous.

There is much about the culture and institutions of Flaubert's times that is mocked in *Bouvard and Pecuchet*. Yet the characters themselves emerge more as objects of affection than of disdain. They are presented as wonderers who might fare better in a differently organised world. Here, as often with Flaubert's novels, it can be difficult to disentangle authorial sympathy from irony. It is helpful to remember a remark he made to Louise Colet, talking of *Madame Bovary*: 'The irony does not detract from the pathetic aspect, but rather intensifies it.'[8]

In letters to George Sand, Flaubert talked with enthusiasm and trepidation of his work in progress on the big book about his 'two woodlice'. The writing, he says in one letter, is giving him terrifying difficulties, yet he would not like to die before completing it. 'Because, after all, it's my testament.'[9] In an earlier letter, he had told her: 'Certainly one has to be absolutely *mad* to undertake such a book. I fear it may be fundamentally impossible – in its very conception. We'll see. Ah! If I can pull it off . . . What a dream!'[10]

The research that went into the book was indeed, like that for all his works, enormous. However, with this one there was an unusual challenge: he had to put himself through all the researches which his indefatigable characters would take on. 'Beside the difficulties of the writing, which are frightful, I have to learn many things of which I'm ignorant. In a month, I hope to be finished with agriculture and gardening. And I'll have done only two thirds of my first chapter!'[11]

What Flaubert saw as making the work his 'testament' was of course not his own enactment of the extensive researches of his characters. Nor was he concerned just to explore the amusing naivety of two eccentric individuals – however engaging that may have been. He was addressing the wider mentality which shaped the clerks' intellectual pursuits. The detail of their researches was necessary in order to provide an aura of authenticity for their passion for learning. It is against the background of the voluminous proliferation of knowledge in their times that the poignancy of their struggles becomes visible.

In other novels, especially *Madame Bovary* and *Sentimental Education*, the targets of Flaubert's ironic observations had been the residue of Romanticism in the consciousness of his contemporaries. In *Bouvard and Pecuchet*, by contrast, he seems to have in his sights the reverberations of an earlier period of thought – Enlightenment ideas of the advancement of humanity through the general diffusion of knowledge. Bouvard and Pecuchet are, by inclination, not mere scholarly pedants. They dream of contributing to social improvement – the transformation of their environment – through knowledge. They are dreamers, but there is often a practical orientation to their dreams. They are inspired by ideals of progress. Their individual projects fail miserably, yet they doggedly keep their faith in the attainability of knowledge and in the social goods its accumulation can deliver.

The most poignant stage in the clerks' adventures – and the most important for our purposes – comes when their insistent self-expression has led to their being labelled by their fellow citizens, no longer as harmlessly eccentric, but as dangerously subversive. The turning point comes when they are seen as beginning 'to cast doubt on the integrity of men, the chastity of women, the wisdom of the government, the common sense of the people'. Their final downfall comes when they are perceived, in short, as undermining the foundations of society. 'Their superiority was painfully obvious and wounded peoples' feelings. As they promoted immoral theses, they must themselves be immoral. Slanderous things were said.'[12]

It is an important moment – both in the structure of the novel and in its bearing on wonder and stupidity. There is a quick stylistic shift there from the authorial voice to 'free indirect speech'. The judgement on the characters does not come from a narrating voice, but from the clerks' hostile critics – though not in a form that would allow of its being attributed to any identifiable observer. It is not clear who judges that the clerks must be immoral. Nor is it clear from whose perspective the things said are 'slanderous'. Breaking through from somewhere there comes this trenchant statement: 'Then their minds developed a piteous faculty, that of perceiving stupidity and being unable to tolerate it.' From that point on, the clerks become indifferent to the state of their world and to their own place within it. 'Bouvard and Pecuchet cared not a whit. The world diminished in importance. They saw it as if through a haze that had drifted down from their brains and over their eyes' (p. 206).

The intolerable insight into stupidity, which has wrought the piteous change in the clerks, is not directed at their own limitations. The brutal reality they have come to see is the closed minds – the collective stupidity – of their fellows. They are now forced to live in a reality imposed on them by the way others perceive them: a reality which is at odds with their own self-perception. What they had previously perceived as their resolute self-expression has now become dangerously subversive. They have become outcasts through their commitment to articulating judgements grounded – however eccentrically – in acquired experience. Here the ideal of social reform through the spread of knowledge confronts the collective stupidity of rigid received opinion. Faced with that hardening resistance, Bouvard and Pecuchet can no longer bear to analyse the information they collect, or to form communicable judgements on its basis. The idea of a shared community of judgement has deserted them.

In the aftermath of that crucial insight, the clerks are no longer just eccentrics pursuing dreams of knowledge. The outcome is indeed piteous. They abandon the challenge of understanding, and become frantic duplicators and preservers of the written word. Unable to deliver the goods promised from the dissemination of knowledge, their desire turns pathetically to the preservation of its material form. The effort to communicate ideas becomes a struggle to proliferate words. In Flaubert's notes for the unwritten concluding chapters, the clerks return to their desks – or, more exactly, to a newly designed single desk with two sides – and resume their original task of copying.

Dreams of advancing human progress through knowledge have been replaced by a different driving passion – the frantic reproduction of whatever piece of written text the clerks can find. 'They copy haphazardly, whatever falls into their hands, all the papers and manuscripts they come across, tobacco packets, old newspapers, lost letters, believing it all to be important and worth preserving.' Faced with the need to introduce some order into that endless material, they 'classify' it by copying it all over into a large business register. They take pleasure in the physical act of copying. Flaubert's notes end with a view of the two heroes leaning over their desk, copying: 'What shall we do with this? – No time for reflection! Let's copy. The page must be filled, the "monument" completed. All things are equal: good and evil, beautiful and ugly, insignificant and characteristic' (pp. 280–1).

The story has come beautifully full circle; but there is much that remains elusive about its upshot. Against the hopes he had expressed to George Sand, Flaubert did die before he had completed the fable of his times, which he had wanted to be his testament. However, for our concern with the work's bearing on the relations between wonder and stupidity, there are useful insights to be gained by its planned juxtaposition with his *Dictionary of Accepted Ideas*, along with a separate *Catalogue of Fashionable Ideas* which also remained uncompleted at his death.

The 'piteous' insight that is the turning point of the novel is complemented by Flaubert's illustrations of the hardening of thought into the clichés of socially legitimated certainty, which he encapsulated in his lists of accepted ideas or received opinions. These assemblages of common sayings cleverly exploit the dictionary format; but, rather than listing accepted meanings, they gather common responses, which have become required parlance in a social group. They are phrases which, through repetitious circulation, have become constitutive parts of a collectively experienced world.

Keeping in mind Flaubert's earlier observations about stupidity, the entries in his lists can be seen as socially predetermined 'conclusions', reached without engagement in the shared intellectual life of communicated thought. They reflect a social world that has closed itself off from the shared activity of conjectural or deliberative thinking – a world closed to the uncertainties of wonder.

Worlds of Books: Giacomo and Anthony

There are some interesting intimations in Flaubert's earliest writings of the thought underlying his connecting of wonder and stupidity. In a very early story, 'Bibliomania', written when he was fourteen, he told the story of Giacomo, a semi-literate monk living in Barcelona, who collects books which he is barely able to read. Giacomo's obsession is focused on books as beautiful objects – described in sensuous detail – and also on their uniqueness. His downfall unfolds in his disillusionment on discovering that a passionately sought version of the Bible is not, as he had thought, the only copy in existence.

Giacomo's mania echoes in the descent of Bouvard and Pecuchet into obsession with preserving the written word. Their original preoccupations were directed, not to the collection of books as beautiful objects, but to acquisition of the knowledge they contain, and to the dream of progress associated with that knowledge. The sad outcome of their passion is a frenzied version of their old humdrum activity as copy clerks, from which they had hoped to escape into the luminous world of learning. Their return to obsessive copying is in some ways the antithesis of – yet in other ways comically similar to – Giacomo's preoccupation with possessing unique literary versions. They have in common an obsession with the written word, which evolves into its complete sundering from understanding, interpretation and judgement.

There are some related – and for our purposes more significant – resonances in *Bouvard and Pecuchet* of another of Flaubert's works, *The Temptations of St Anthony*. Flaubert wrote three versions of it, reworking the final one after he had already begun work on *Bouvard and Pecuchet*. At first sight, the two works seem worlds apart – one, a series of horrifying apparitions experienced by a third-century anchorite; the other, a comic tale of modern aspirations for knowledge. Yet in a letter to George Sand he described his final work as a book 'of the same stamp' as the *Temptations*.[13] He had, in an earlier letter to Sand, already talked of *Bouvard and Pecuchet* as a 'modern' novel which, despite its 'comic' genre, would be 'a counterpoint to *Saint Antoine*'.[14]

Flaubert had long been intrigued by a Breughel painting of Anthony's temptations. He wrote to Colet of the pleasure he took in the 'immense charm' of the 'tragic grotesque' which the picture exerted on him. He found in it something 'buffoonishly bitter', which answered to his sense of his own nature: 'It doesn't make me laugh, but sets me dreaming. I recognise it wherever it exists.'[15] It is an early expression of an idea to which Flaubert often returned in his reflections on Art and Truth – of a state he calls 'reverie', which has much in common with wonder. In a later letter to Colet, he says: 'What seems to me the highest and most difficult achievement of Art is not to make us laugh or cry, nor to arouse our lust or rage, but to do what nature does – that is, to set us dreaming.'[16] Flaubert's 'reverie' stands to artistic consciousness in a similar relation to that in which some forms of scepticism stand to belief. It is a withholding of commitment – a kind of detachment, which can nonetheless involve a deep attentiveness.

The recurring idea of a kind of perception that sees things as 'just there' is in the background of Flaubert's reflections on the two works which simultaneously occupied his attention; yet what exactly he saw as connecting them remained somewhat opaque in his comments. One story confronts and challenges the certainties of Christian belief; the other, the vagaries of an Enlightenment mentality. Yet they do have some elements in common: the circulation of knowledge through the reproduction of books; the idea of encyclopaedic learning encompassed in a particular culture; temptation – or at any rate frailty – induced by a sense of alienation from conventional orthodoxies; an extended series of trials; the interplay of belief and illusion, and its possible descent into ongoing delusion.

Michel Foucault has offered some illuminating insights into the works' common concern with books and literacy, in his essay 'Fantasies in the Library'. He points out that the literary form of the final version of the *Temptations* relies on its location within the domain of knowledge: the work exists by virtue of its essential relation to books. For Foucault that is why the work represents more than a mere episode in the history of the western imagination: 'It opens a literary space wholly dependent on the network formed by the books of the past.' Flaubert, he argues, has here extended the imaginative spaces that actually existing books can occupy. It is a book which 'recovers other books' – 'hides and displays them and, in a single movement . . . causes them to glitter and disappear'.[17] In that respect, Foucault concludes, the *Temptations* 'seems to summon *Bouvard and Pecuchet*, at least to the extent that the latter stands as its grotesque shadow, its tiny yet boundless double' (p. 107).

Bouvard and Pecuchet, on Foucault's reading, seek knowledge in a very different imaginative space from Anthony. The *Temptations* works by transforming a multiplicity of books into a dramatic succession of striking images. The saint is exposed to a pantomime-like series of bizarre hallucinations – a dazzling array of figures from the history of cultures, philosophies and religions. The apparitions do not refer back directly to their sources; there is no logical progression in the 'temptations' they pose. In *Bouvard and Pecuchet*, in contrast, the source library is clearly visible – classified and analysed. 'The fantastic is no longer a property of the heart, nor is it found among the incongruities of nature; it evolves from the accuracy of knowledge, and its treasures lie dormant in documents' (p. 90).

Foucault's reading centres on the predicaments of belief within two very different social organisations of knowledge. Bouvard and Pecuchet are entranced by their books, but they are not reduced to passivity by them, as Anthony is before the onslaught of his picturesque phantoms. The clerks are indefatigable pilgrims of learning, trying out everything they touch, putting everything to the test of their industrious application. On Foucault's interpretation, their 'temptation' arises from their zeal. 'For these two simple men, to be tempted is to believe. It is to believe in the things they read, to believe in the things they overhear; it is to believe immediately and unquestioningly in the persistent flow of discourse' (p. 107). Their successive obsessions involve an inability to resist 'temptations' to believe.

These are suggestive readings, which open up other possibilities for contemporary applications. Anthony is exposed to the perils of uncertainty when one treasured set of certainties is exposed to rival belief systems. The grotesque apparitions challenge his confidence in his habitual strong convictions of the unique truth of Christianity. From a broader secular perspective, that loss might well be seen as liberation. Anthony has gained the freedom to delight in the sheer variety of knowledge systems, without being limited by commitment to any one of them. Unsurprisingly, though – as a man of his time – he experiences this superfluity of possibilities, not as an exhilarating release, but as anguish at the threatened loss of treasured certainty.

The apparitions are described in sensuous detail which intensifies the terror, but their force as 'temptations' comes from their intellectual content. The horror centres on a loss of conviction in the exclusive truth of the Christian beliefs around which Anthony has structured his life. The images offer tantalising intellectual and spiritual pleasures, which entice him to embrace new ways of living. He is drawn towards acting out possibilities from which his Christian commitments had hitherto excluded him. Flaubert has given this Anthony a nineteenth-century consciousness, forced into an ancient character mould.

Thus, the possibility that a conviction might be so strong that one might die for it now becomes, for Anthony, not a noble hope of martyrdom, but a source of torment. He grasps the possibility that others might happily die for belief systems different from those to which he has directed his ascetic life. He turns for reassurance to his awareness of miracles which have uniquely authenticated his Christian faith, only to find that other systems can claim with equanimity a similar justification. The certainties of faith give way to the instabilities of wavering belief. If all can carry equal conviction, then none can lay claim to his commitment.

Anthony faces the realisation that belief systems other than his own can be both persuasive and beautiful – and that his own can be no less violent and vile than others. He is terrified by these endless possibilities of competing truths. Yet the thought that all may be completed – that there may be no more possibilities for belief – brings fresh dismay: when all has been accomplished, perhaps all that remains is destruction.

The sense of dread associated with the sublime in Romantic Idealist thought was accompanied by a persistent yearning for the unattainable. In contrast, Flaubert's Anthony is left with the hopelessness of the idea that all possibilities have been exhausted. The *Temptations* is a narrative of the dissolution of all belief, which dramatises the potential disillusionment lurking in every creed. Anthony's religious commitments are challenged as he is exposed to a plethora of alternative models of virtue and vice, heroism and villainy. The work explores the implications for religious faith of the modern explosion of accessible knowledge; but it also engages with broader issues of the nature of conviction – of its vulnerability when confronted with alternative possibilities; of the inherent uncertainty of belief.

The adventures and misadventures of Bouvard and Pecuchet enact a predicament of modern knowledge which is comparable to that of Flaubert's Anthony – a surfeit of possibilities, when the whole of human history becomes available to consciousness. The clerks, to their delight, unexpectedly find themselves with the wherewithal to learn about, and act out, the apparently endless possibilities opened up by the availability of books. There is, for them, an additional hazard in that availability of knowledge. As lovers of learning, shaped in a post-Enlightenment mentality, they want to draw from their books productive activity directed to the well-being of their fellows. They are vulnerable not only to the inherent uncertainties of belief, but also to the inevitable uncertainty of outcomes.

These characters have more enthusiasm than wisdom, and their dabbling has some unfortunate results – for others as well as for themselves. Yet, in the end, they are more victims of stupidity than perpetrators of it. What stays with us is Flaubert's account of their 'piteous' insights into the intolerable collective stupidity that makes them outcasts – the stupidity that resides in the forces which bring wonder to a premature end. It was this aspect of *Bouvard and Pecuchet*, as we will see, that most engaged the interest of Deleuze and Derrida. It was also central to a notorious interpretation of Flaubert offered by Jean-Paul Sartre.

Sartre on Flaubert

Sartre framed his study of Flaubert, *The Family Idiot*, as an attempt to read the author's life through his times, while also treating the life as expressive of those times.[18] In his Preface to the work, he remarks that a man is never just an individual – it would be more fitting to call him a *universal singular*. An individual man, he says, is 'universalised by his epoch'; and that epoch is epitomised, in turn, by being reproduced in his singularity. Sartre's project, then, is to reconfigure Flaubert's individual life as the product of history. Towards the end of the first volume, he pursues that theme through an extended discussion of a form of stupidity. Strangely, it is both appropriated from Flaubert and projected onto him as an instantiation of the concept.

The French term *bêtise* carries a suggestion that the English 'stupidity' lacks: to be *bêtise* is to be – at least for a while – something less than human, something animal-like. It calls to mind the lack of something which has, throughout the western philosophical tradition, been taken as a defining characteristic of being human: reason – the capacity of intellect to order experience through general terms. *Bêtise* has connotations of a perilous descent into the realm the beast – of mere 'particularity', untransformed by universal concepts.

Of course, the occasional bit of stupid behaviour does not warrant – either in English or in French – an attribution of stupidity as an ongoing disposition. Yet the associations of *bêtise* with an absence of humanity – however fleeting – do seem to suggest a major risk for the thinking mind. The state of *bêtise* is, by its very description, something best avoided. Yet there is also a striking resemblance between the condition it evokes – of being thrust into a confrontation with untranscended particularity – and traditional accounts of wonder. It is those connections that intrigue Sartre, and later Derrida, in relation to Flaubert's concern with *bêtise*.

The Family Idiot is an ambitious work, and in some ways a preposterous one. Sartre makes audacious leaps between common ways of thinking and individual psychic structures. Flaubert's intellectual character is analysed through family relations – most importantly through his relatives' perceptions of him as stupid. On Sartre's imaginative reconstruction, the child viewed words from the outside – as having the solidity of *things*, even when they are inside him. The impenetrability the young Flaubert encountered in his struggles to master the letters of the alphabet was part of a broader lack of connection with the normal intersubjectivity of language. He experienced words as an external alien force.

This supposedly stupid child was at the same time a curious and astute observer of adult inanities. On Sartre's analysis, there is a connection between that early fascination with stupidities and the child's difficulties with language. His apparent stupidity is associated with an oppressive sense of a 'thickening' of language, which forms between mind and world, and also between minds. The child's sense of his own stupidity – imposed on him by the way he was seen by significant others – develops in tandem with his observations of the stupidities which surround him. For Sartre, the perceived stupidity of the child, his reciprocal perceptions of adult stupidities, and his sense of himself as stupid, are all interconnected.

Sartre's reconstruction of Flaubert's childhood highlights a letter he wrote at the age of nine to a young friend, in which he talks of the tedious exchanges between adults at ritualised celebrations, and of his interest in collecting examples of such stupidities: 'If you'd like us to work together at writing, I'll write comedies and you can write your dreams, and since there's a lady who comes to see papa and always says stupid things I'll write them too.'[19]

The sentiments habitually expressed at family gatherings are perceived by the child as mindless conventional responses. The adult Flaubert remained convinced that he was surrounded by reiterated stupidities. That opinion, Sartre comments, was not unusual among nineteenth-century French intellectuals – to be bourgeois, they thought, was to be philistine. However, they typically saw stupidity as an absence, a privation of intelligence; those afflicted by it were considered harmful only to themselves. What made Flaubert's attitude to stupidity distinctive was that he saw it as an external force – a source of oppression. As Sartre summed it up, for Flaubert, 'the fool became an oppressor'. It is an insight that helps make sense of the 'piteous' state into which Bouvard and Pecuchet are thrown when they realise they have become social outcasts: they become passive under the oppressive force of the mindless judgements of others. Sartre, however, takes the idea further. Flaubert himself, he argues, interiorised the perceptions of others, so that he became his own oppressor.

According to Sartre, Flaubert's project in the *Dictionary of Accepted Ideas* is to be understood in the light of his lifelong preoccupation with stupidity. The passion for collecting inanities, displayed by a precociously observant child, persists into the adult author's caustic assemblage of conventional responses. What the child called 'stupid things people say', the adult comes to describe as 'accepted ideas'. However, Sartre again goes further, taking Flaubert himself to be enacting the kind of thinking his Dictionary exemplifies.

Sartre points out, correctly, that Flaubert's collection of 'received ideas' is curiously disparate: the compilation observes no real distinction between ready-made ideas and conventional sentiments. Failures of emotional intelligence are included, along with reiterations of uncritical opinions. Rather than classifying the citations, Flaubert simply lists them alphabetically: 'Accepted ideas, locutions, puns and wordplays, "gems" are all jumbled together' (p. 627). Sometimes the entry includes an imperative as to what attitude a listener is expected to adopt: 'BACCALAUREATE: Thunder against it.' 'DOCTRINARIANS: Despise them. Why? No idea.' Other entries appear as statements of fact. Among these, some are simply common mistakes, from ignorance; others are facetiously presented as Flaubert's own opinions.

Sartre sees in Flaubert's Dictionary a flawed realisation of the intersubjective character of the spoken word. In the lack of the shared spontaneity facilitated by free-flowing language, the collecting of clichés comes to evoke passivity and inertia. 'This stupidity is infinite, because it possesses the impassability and impenetrability of natural facts' (p. 602). It is, Sartre says, as if language has become 'materiality aping thought' or 'thought haunting matter'. According to Sartre, language, of itself, is for Flaubert nothing but stupidity. Verbal materiality, left to itself, 'produces a kind of thought-matter'. On Sartre's diagnosis, this wavering between thought and matter is the explanation of Flaubert's 'double attitude' towards stupidity – sometimes fascinated, sometimes repelled by it – 'both an abyss that makes him dizzy and the weight of the whole world oppressing him'. Flaubert wants to escape from stupidity, yet he dreams of 'taking upon himself all the stupidity of the world' (p. 610).

Given his emphasis on the materiality of stupidity – its emulation of the status of 'things' – it is not surprising that Sartre is drawn to those letters in which Flaubert himself used some strikingly concrete metaphors to capture its oppressive force. Writing to a friend of a visit to Egypt in 1850, he says: 'Stupidity is something unshakeable, nothing can attack it without being broken. It has the quality of granite, hard and resistant.' He sardonically recalls having seen, in Alexandria, how 'a certain

Thompson from Sunderland' had written his name in letters six feet high on Pompeii's column: 'This imbecile has become a part of the monument and is perpetuated with it.' All fools, Flaubert laments, are more or less like Thompson from Sunderland, and they always get the better of us. 'On a trip you meet a lot of them . . . but they soon go away; you are amused by them. It's not like ordinary life, when they manage to drive you crazy!'[20]

Sartre's critique of Flaubert's Dictionary goes well beyond concern with its lexicographical limitations. He extracts from it a kind of thinking which he sees as exemplified in the persona he has constructed as 'Flaubert'. This 'Flaubert' is taken as instantiating the form of stupidity which Flaubert – the real Flaubert – helped to expose. Sartre complains that his Flaubert never succeeds in transcending the commonplaces he derides, by turning them to serve his own purposes; that he confines himself to discrediting opinions by setting them against one another. Rather than breaking through the banalities to express fresh thought, he takes refuge in scepticism; he is careful not to form any ideas of his own.

This retreat to scepticism is the interpretation Sartre puts on Flaubert's own elusive, but suggestive, equating of stupidity with 'wanting to reach a conclusion'. With him, says Sartre, 'thought is never an act, it invents nothing, it never establishes connections: it is not distinguishable from the movement of life itself'. In brief, he concludes, Flaubert is a martyr to stupidity; he has 'taken it into himself, with all its conflicts: it turns and, devouring itself, devours him as well' (pp. 625–6).

Sartre's derisory comments on Flaubert's style of thinking are surely overstated. His *Family Idiot* is closer to imaginative fiction – with some help from his own philosophy – than to literary biography. Yet there are interesting insights here into the form of stupidity that Flaubert tried to expose. 'In effect', Sartre says, 'stupidity is decapitated reason, it is the intellectual operation deprived of its unity, in other words, of its power of unification'. Failing to achieve — or perhaps even to desire — that unifying capacity of reason, such stupidity remains immersed in 'the animal consciousness of the world', reduced to 'the pure boredom of living' which seems especially to be 'the lot of domestic animals' (p. 627). Rather than conceding this 'Flaubert' the intellectually respectable status of the sceptic, Sartre seems, perversely, to condemn him to mere 'animal' awareness — an almost literal form of *bêtise*.

The understanding of stupidity — especially under its French terminology — has exerted a fascination in recent times for the philosophical imagination. In Chapter 7 we will see Gilles Deleuze and Jacques Derrida pursue it, 'following the track of Flaubert'. First, however, we need to address different tracks, along which contemporary philosophers have tried to reconnect with aspects of older ways of construing states associated with wonder.

Notes

1 Gustave Flaubert, *Correspondance*, 9 vols (Paris: Conard, 1926–33), Vol. II, p. 398; quoted in Jonathan Culler, *Flaubert: The Uses of Uncertainty* (Aurora: Davies Group, 1984), p. 175.
2 Letter to Colet, 11 January 1847, in *The Letters of Gustave Flaubert 1830–1857*, ed. and trans. Francis Steegmuller (London: Faber and Faber, 1980), p. 89.
3 Flaubert, *Correspondance*, Vol. III, p. 37; quoted in Culler, *Flaubert: The Uses of Uncertainty*, p. 63.
4 Letter of 4 September 1850, in *The Letters of Gustave Flaubert*, p. 128.
5 Gustave Flaubert, *Madame Bovary*, trans. Adam Thorp (London: Vintage

Books, 2012), p. 154. Further page references will be given in the main text.
6 Letter to Colet, 8–9 August 1846, in *The Letters of Gustave Flaubert*, p. 52.
7 Letter to Colet, 9 December 1852, in *The Letters of Gustave Flaubert*, p. 173.
8 Letter of 9 October 1852, in *The Letters of Gustave Flaubert*, p. 172.
9 Letter to Sand, 18 February 1876, in Gustave Flaubert, *The Correspondence of Gustave Flaubert and George Sand*, trans. Francis Steegmuller and Barbara Bray (London: The Harvill Press, 1999), p. 390.
10 Letter to Sand, 26 September 1874, in *The Correspondence of Gustave Flaubert and George Sand*, p. 353.
11 Letter to Sand, 2 December 1874, in *The Correspondence of Gustave Flaubert and George Sand*, p. 358
12 Gustave Flaubert, *Bouvard and Pecuchet* [1881], trans. Mark Polizzotti (Dalkey Archive Press, 2005), p. 205. Further page references will be given in the main text.
13 Letter of 1 May 1874, in *The Correspondence of Gustave Flaubert and George Sand*, p. 344.
14 Letter of 1 July 1872, in *The Correspondence of Gustave Flaubert and George Sand*, p. 277.
15 Letter of 21–2 August 1846, in *The Letters of Gustave Flaubert*, p. 68.
16 Letter of 26 August 1853, in *The Letters of Gustave Flaubert*, p. 198.
17 Michel Foucault, 'Fantasies of the Library', in *Language, Counter-Memory, Practice: Selected Essays and Interviews*, ed. Donald F. Bouchard (Ithaca: Cornell University Press, 1977), pp. 91–2. Further page references will be given in the main text.
18 Jean-Paul Sartre, *The Family Idiot: Gustave Flaubert 1821–1857*, Vol. I, trans. Carol Cosman (Chicago: University of Chicago Press, 1981). Further page references will be given in the main text.
19 Letter to Ernest Chevalier, before January 1831, in *The Letters of Gustave Flaubert*, p. 3; quoted in Sartre, *The Family Idiot*, p. 594.
20 Flaubert, *Correspondance*, Vol. II, p. 243; quoted in Culler, *Flaubert: The Uses of Uncertainty*, p. 175.

6

Reconnecting with Socratic Wonder: Heidegger and Arendt

We may no longer think of *ourselves* as sublime. Yet we can still respond to the emotional power of the concept, even if we cannot see it as central to our understanding of who we are. The sublime still resonates in our responses to scenes of wildness and grandeur, and it still epitomises awe and admiration in the evaluation of art and literature. But the continued intelligibility and appeal of the sublime as an aesthetic notion does not minimise the sense of loss of connection, in relation to older ways of thinking of – and with – wonder. More recent philosophy has seen some significant efforts to reconnect with some of that lost centrality of wonder to thinking.

As the old connections between wonder and intellectual inquiry became attenuated, a long-standing ambivalence was able to harden into more explicit mistrust or disdain. With wonder absorbed into the sublime – now the domain of art or poetry – philosophical concern with wonder could be relegated to aesthetic theory. Kant's emphasis on the unity of the mind's faculties had brought aesthetic judgement into relation with theoretical and practical reason, as well as with imagination. The weakening of that sense of a harmonising between mental faculties left the sense of the sublime disconnected from other aspects of the life of the mind. With wonder no longer regarded as central to inquiry, its connections with imagination could more readily come to be seen as primarily concerned with the construction of fictions. Wonder then comes to belong with the creation of fictional objects, rather than with the understanding of what is objectively *there*. It becomes a stimulus to the generation of fantasies, while remaining nonetheless a powerful emotional response to Nature.

Wonder has been conceded a place in contemporary consciousness: there is, after all, a thriving market for fantasy literature. Yet, having come adrift from its old connections with intellectual inquiry, it has also largely lost its place in the understanding of reality. In the early twentieth century, Martin Heidegger attempted to restore to wonder something of its old status by reconnecting it with its Socratic past.

Heidegger on Wonder at the Ordinary

Heidegger made only passing reference to wonder in elaborating his central concept of *Dasein*, in his best-known work *Being and Time*, published in 1927. It has, however, an important place in the related account of *attunement*, which he offered in the sections on 'World', 'Finitude' and 'Solitude' in his 1929–30 lecture course, published in 1983 as *The Fundamental Concepts of Metaphysics*. He later spelled out the ramifications of those reflections in a more direct discussion of wonder in his later lecture course of 1937–8, published in 1984 as *Basic Questions of Philosophy*.

In his treatment of wonder, Heidegger is concerned to rethink the nature of the intellectual activity involved in philosophical thought. That activity, he argues, happens in a fundamental *attunement* – a distinctive 'disposition' which sets philosophy apart from scientific inquiry. The term is intended to give content to an idea that Novalis had expressed poetically in saying that philosophy is really 'homesickness' – an urge to be at home everywhere. Heidegger links his account of wonder with a rejection of the idea that certainty is the appropriate goal of philosophical thinking. Philosophy, he says, is 'the opposite of all comfort and assurance'. Vacillation is a precondition for this kind of thinking; and the rejection of comfort makes philosophical thinking 'ultimate and extreme'.

The concept of *attunement* is meant to reflect this repudiation of certainty as the goal of philosophical thinking, and with it the model of the philosopher as directing a clear gaze to the inspection of mental states. An *attunement* does not appear in the mind as an object capable of being inspected for distinguishing marks. It is not a particular being; it is rather a fundamental *manner* of being. Heidegger's *attunements* are fundamental ways in which we find ourselves *disposed*. They are not states of mind we inspect, but rather conditions – ways of being – in which we find ourselves.[1]

It is an indirect route that we are asked to follow from there to the understanding of wonder. Heidegger begins by challenging a familiar model of philosophical inquiry into mental states, according to which a mental object comes before the observing mind, which conducts a painstaking inspection before delivering a definitive account of it. In what is perhaps the most famous instantiation of this model, Descartes, in his *Meditations*, presents himself as carefully inspecting 'ideas' for distinguishing marks of 'clarity' and 'distinctness', which will serve as criteria of certainty. A similar model operates, though less rigidly, in his accounts in the *Passions of the Soul* of specific emotions, including wonder. A comparable approach is taken in Spinoza's descriptions of emotional states in the *Ethics*. He has rejected the Cartesian programme of finding certainty through the rigorous inspection of inner mental states. Yet the geometrical form of the *Ethics* imposes on his own treatment of the emotions an implicit model of an attentive mind seeking defining characteristics of objects brought before it.

Heidegger takes a different approach to the understanding of emotions. It is in some ways akin to an exploration of what Spinoza called the imagination's 'inadequate' ideas of body, rather than to the definitions he sought in more 'adequate' ideas. Rather than evoking a clear-thinking knowing subject, confronting an as yet indeterminate object, Heidegger offers us an account of the whole experience of coming to understand situations imbued with emotion. His resort to the notion of *attunement* is central to that shift of model; it is the key to understanding 'lived experience'. An *attunement*, in this usage, does not appear before the mind as an object to be inspected for distinguishing marks. Hence his insistence that it is not a particular determinate being, but rather a *manner* of being.

Heidegger fills out the content of this notion of *attunement* through a fascinating – though laborious – analysis of the condition of boredom. Boredom may well seem the antithesis of the entrancing intensity associated with wonder – especially in the experience of the sublime. However, Heidegger's discussion of boredom brings out many points of connection between it and traditional accounts of wonder. He offers three illustrations: first, boredom *in* a tiresome situation – as in prolonged waiting for a train; second, being bored *with* a situation – as with a disappointing social occasion that we had expected to enjoy; third, what he calls 'profound' boredom – a more generalised state, in which something is 'boring as such'. In this third way, he says, something is boring for an undifferentiated 'one'. This is a boredom which arises, not from any particular situation, but rather where we are delivered back to 'the point where all and everything appears indifferent to us' (p. 137).

He stresses that all three cases involve exposure to the human experience of temporality. Time itself is here presented as somehow constituting the concealed essence of boredom. He plays with etymological links in the German language to develop his point. Boredom is *Langeweile*, longness of time; and experiencing that also means the same as being 'homesick'. Drawing, as he says, on 'the wisdom of language' – while not thereby using it as an authority – he emphasises that time 'becomes long' in boredom; we are prompted to 'pass the time' in order to master its 'longness'. What is involved is a 'shortening' that drives on the time that seeks to become long. 'Passing the time' is here not meant to connote distraction or diversion. It is meant, rather, to suggest intervention or disruption. It is the experience of boredom that is being described, not any suggested practical remedy. The mind intervenes in order to drive on 'the time that seeks to become long' (p. 96).

We may be unimpressed, or even exasperated, by the verbal play; but there is an important insight here: boredom is not simply an inner object, demanding of us a description or definition. It is, Heidegger insists, 'much rather the case that boredom is outside, seated in what is boring, and creeps into us from the outside' (p. 83). What emerges is that boredom both 'belongs to the object' and is, at the same time, 'related to the subject'. This hybrid character is an important general feature of what Heidegger calls *attunements*: they are 'partly objective, partly subjective' (p. 88). To be thus 'attuned' is the fundamental nature of human comportment towards the world. That condition is captured in his complex concept of *Dasein*, which also involves the entrancing power of time.

How does this bear on wonder? Heidegger stresses the sense of something 'indeterminate' and 'unfamiliar' which characterises what is boring: the sense of strangeness – of 'I know not what'. We must, he insists, hang onto that if we want to understand the experience of boredom (p. 119). The sense of strangeness and indeterminacy has been a recurring theme in philosophical discussion of wonder. So, too, has been the sense of a pause in mental activity – verging on a dislocation from the ordinary flow of time. Although his main concern here, in the lectures on World, Finitude and Solitude, is to illustrate the notion of *attunement* through consideration of the condition of boredom, Heidegger's observations on time also prepare the way for his account of wonder, which he will address in the later lecture course, published as *Basic Questions of Philosophy*.

The connections between this strangeness and the human experience of temporality become clearer when Heidegger moves on to discuss more fully the ways in which *attunement* involves a 'comportment' towards being. This is what gives content to the rich 'world-forming' capacity that distinguishes the human from the 'world-poor animal' and the 'worldless' stone. Having a 'world' depends on being able to experience temporality. For Heidegger, this capacity involves in turn a sense of mortality – a 'comportment towards one's own death'. 'Man always comports himself somehow or other towards death, that is, towards *his* death' (p. 294).

Heidegger is careful here to distinguish this orientation towards death from any idea of a constant dwelling on mortality.

He rejects as a misinterpretation the idea that 'running ahead towards death' constitutes the 'proper authenticity of human existence'. It is not as if, in order to 'exist properly', human beings must be constantly thinking about death. If we attempt to do that, he comments, then we will be unable to endure existence at all; the only way to achieve such a supposedly 'authentic existence' would be to commit suicide. To thus seek the essence of our proper existence in its annihilation would be, he says, a conclusion 'as insane as it is absurd'.

There is, nonetheless, a kind of perilousness in Heidegger's own version of what he calls 'comportment towards death' which – perhaps surprisingly – gives his treatment of boredom some resonance with the idea of the sublime. This form of thinking has a dark side, which evokes the sense of dread associated with the sublime, as well as older ideas of philosophy as 'beginning in wonder'. 'Only where there is the perilousness of being seized by terror do we find the bliss of astonishment – being torn away in that wakeful manner that is the breath of all philosophizing' (p. 366). In his later lecture course, of 1937–8, those resonances become more prominent, lending a distinctive tone to his version of philosophical thinking.

The language in which Heidegger describes philosophical thinking is evocative of intense emotion. Yet, early on in the later lectures, he insists that the basic disposition of this kind of thinking is an attitude of 'restraint', arising from the interaction of two elements which are 'as one': 'terror in the face of what is closest and most obtrusive, namely that beings are', and 'awe in the face of what is remotest, namely that in beings, and before each being, Being holds sway'. Restraint, in this form, is 'the disposition in which this terror is not overcome and set aside but is precisely preserved and conserved through awe'.[2]

Although Heidegger does not in these lectures directly discuss the feeling of the sublime, there are echoes of it in this convergence of awe and terror. Yet he is eager to distance himself from any interpretation of his treatment of philosophical thinking which would associate it with states of exalted experience. He insists that what philosophical thinking demands is, above all, 'reflection'. His elaboration of this state of non-exalted reflection brings us, at last, to wonder. Heidegger's version of it draws on ancient Greek ideas, which he renders as 'openness' – or 'unconcealedness' – as the proper essence of truth (p. 88).

Heidegger claims that modern thought has come to operate with a shrunken, diminished understanding of the concept of truth. It has shed one of the two senses of truth with which the ancient Greeks were acquainted. They thought of truth, firstly, in terms of the notion of 'unconcealedness' or the 'openness' of beings; and, secondly, as 'correctness' – the assimilation of a representation to those directly apprehended beings (p. 95). He argues that the first sense of truth has been largely discarded in modern thought, leaving truth to be construed exclusively as 'the correctness of judging reason' (p. 90). The ancient philosophers, on Heidegger's reconstruction of them, saw truth as a characteristic of beings themselves, rather than – as in the ordinary view of later times – 'a matter of assertions about beings' (p. 102).

Heidegger's talk of a kind of thinking suffused with 'perilousness' may sound like older accounts of the feeling of the sublime; but he makes it clear in these lectures in *Basic Questions of Philosophy* that it is for him a reconnection with something much older – grounded in an ancient Greek way of thinking of truth. What exactly is this 'perilousness', then, and how does it relate to wonder? Heidegger's answer comes through a reconsideration of the related idea of *aporia*. The mental distress occasioned by 'not knowing the way out or the way in', which the Greeks connected with the origins of philosophy, is for Heidegger a distinctive form of perplexity – deeper than any specific state of puzzlement. He stresses that, although we now translate what they called *thaumazein* as 'wonder', we should not assume that it is indeed the same condition. We must be willing to go back to try to engage with what *thaumazein* originally was – to clarify the 'basic disposition' of that 'beginning of thinking' (p. 135).

Thus, as Heidegger sees it, when the ancient Greeks made 'not-knowing' integral to philosophical thinking, what they were talking about was not the 'empty formula of pedantry' to which it has been reduced in modern times. What they called *thaumazein* was something deeper than mere lack of knowledge. If we want to call it 'wonder', we must, he says, first think about the meanings of that word – not as mere lexicography, but in an effort to see something of the inner multiplicity of this 'basic disposition'. This exercise, he insists, is also very different from trying to clarify the psychology of wonder. If we think of the Greeks as relating the beginnings of philosophy to a psychological state similar to 'marvelling', then we only trivialise what they saw as philosophy – depriving it of what is really most distinctive about it. 'To say philosophy originates in wonder means philosophy is wondrous in its essence and becomes more wondrous the more it becomes what it really is' (p. 141).

The wondrous form of wonder that Heidegger finds in the ancient Greek sources may well seem to become more elusive the more he insists on what it is not. He claims that it is different from all types and levels of amazement, admiration and astonishment. Again, there is no explicit mention here of the sublime, but it is clear that much of the language in which the notion of the sublime was expressed would fall under Heidegger's embargo on construing *thaumazein* as a psychological state. Heidegger is here repudiating – as candidates for the putative beginnings of philosophy – not only the sublime, but also less exalted states of surprise. To grasp what is at stake here, it is helpful again to return briefly to Spinoza's treatment of wonder.

On Spinoza's account, the object of wonder is not yet known. Initially, it cannot be assimilated to other things by being brought under general concepts. That is to say, the object of wonder is 'singular'. Yet what is, in Spinoza's sense, 'singular' can at least be identified as something different from other things – something unusual. From Heidegger's perspective, that is to treat the thing wondered at as being a determinate something – even if we don't yet know exactly *what* it is. Whether we are merely 'surprised' or more seriously 'astonished', we can – on that approach – at least see that the thing in question is a determinate something-or-other. 'A determinate individual object stands out as being unusual and distinguishes itself with regard to an equally determinate sphere of what is experienced precisely as usual' (p. 144).

Heidegger's point about such analyses is that, whether we are astonished or merely surprised by singularity, to construe wonder in terms of singularity is to see it as involving a 'turning away from the usual'. What is usual is then left alone – 'bypassed' in its usualness (p. 144). For Heidegger, in contrast, what is distinctive in the wonder of the ancient Greeks is that it does not 'bypass' the usual.

What Heidegger thinks he has found in the ancient Greek sources is a way of attending to what is most usual, so that it becomes – for us – unusual. For those Greek thinkers, what is commonly regarded as so usual that it is – in its usualness – not even noticed, becomes an object of wonder. Heidegger argues that, in reviving this ancient form of wonder, we render the usual unusual, rather than simply bypassing it. He goes on to point out that what we, in modern times, have come to think of as wonder is dissipated by explanation. That is indeed, as we have seen, a familiar motif in modern approaches to wonder: it triggers the desire to know, but is then left behind by the satisfaction of that desire. Heidegger argues that the form of wonder extolled by the ancient Greeks was in that respect very different. He articulates the contrast in a striking reprise of the old metaphor of *aporia* as the lack of a path forward:

> While wonder must venture out into the most extreme unusualness of everything, it is at the same time cast back wholly on itself, knowing that it is incapable of penetrating the unusualness by way of explanation, since that would precisely be to destroy it. Wonder knows no way into the unusualness of what is most usual of all, as little as it knows a way out – it is simply placed before the usualness of the usual, in the midst of the usual in everything. (p. 145)

Continuing to play with – and perhaps overextend – the metaphor of the lost path, while blocking off yet another route to possible clarity, Heidegger insists that this state of 'not knowing the way out or the way in' is not to be construed as helplessness. 'Wonder as such does not desire help but instead precisely opens up this between, which is impervious to any entrance or escape, and must constantly occupy it.' We may well be left wondering – in a more usual sense – how we might know that we are 'between' rather than pursuing some false path of entry or escape. The kind of thinking associated with this version of wonder is supposed to involve a 'thoughtful questioning' quite different from the 'intrusive and rash curiosity of the search for explanations'. This questioning demands tolerating and sustaining 'the unexplainable as such'. It is to be distinguished from 'the avidity for learning and calculation'. Yet nor is it to be construed as 'a vague and empty wallowing in "feelings"' (pp. 148–9).

At the end of these intricate qualifications, it may well seem that to try to sustain Heideggerian wonder would be an exacting, and potentially exasperating, project. Can it really be this complicated to try to reconnect with ancient Greek wonder and philosophising? Heidegger insists that it should not be construed as a psychological state of 'marvelling'. Yet it seems to be imbued with an awe whose intensity – directed though it is at the usual – rivals that of the post-Kantian sublime. There are, nonetheless, some important insights to be gained from Heidegger's careful and eloquent – though at times overwhelming – descriptions. His account of *attunement* – as a hybrid of subjective thought and objective world – opens up fresh possibilities for reflecting on what has become of wonder, even if the path he tracks back to its ancient sources may seem unduly tortuous.

The cast of mind that Heidegger describes as 'thoughtful questioning' suggests an attitude of active awe. Wonder, thus construed, recognises the disturbing force of the mysterious within the everyday, while retaining a detachment which sets it apart from the emotional turmoil associated with the sublime. Clearly, he intends this reconstructed wonder to be very different from the state Descartes disdained as unthinking stupor. It is also meant to involve an intellectual mood very different from the feverish drive to amass knowledge of marvellous things, associated with the old 'cabinets of wonder'.

From a Cartesian perspective, we might ask, unsympathetically, whether it is better to 'gape' at everything – and nothing in particular – rather than just at the unusual. Yet, if we step back from Heidegger's own tortuous path to the 'between', and reflect on the form of wonder he has identified, there is something about it which is familiar from the experience of asking a certain kind of philosophical question. Ludwig Wittgenstein talked of it in a lecture on ethics, originally delivered in Cambridge in 1929: 'I believe the best way of describing it is to say that when I have it I wonder at the existence of the world. And then I am inclined to use such phrases as "How extraordinary that anything should exist" or "How extraordinary that the world should exist."'[3]

Wittgenstein claimed that the verbal expression we give to such an experience is strictly nonsense – that it is a misuse of language to say that I wonder *at* the existence of something which I cannot imagine not existing. Yet he insists that the experience itself is something readily intelligible. There are similarities between Wittgenstein's description of that experience and the condition Heidegger describes as *'wondering-at-Being'*, though Wittgenstein goes on to make observations about its connection with religion, which Heidegger would not endorse.

Heidegger has raised interesting possibilities for reconnection with the engaged thoughtfulness of Socratic wonder. Yet questions remain about the apparent separation of this version of wonder from all desire for explanation, and about whether Heidegger's restatement of a distinctively 'philosophical' style of thinking might bring its own dangerous kind of withdrawal from 'the ordinary'.

Arendt on Wonder and Judgement

The strengths – and the hazards – of Heidegger's wonder-at-the-ordinary were later explored by Hannah Arendt. In an essay marking Heidegger's eightieth birthday, published in the *New York Review of Books* in 1971, she expressed ambivalence about his efforts to reconstruct the kind of philosophical thinking which the ancient Greek philosophers had seen as beginning in wonder.[4] She welcomed his celebration of Socratic wonder, commenting that, in the *Theaetetus*, Plato was the first, and perhaps the only ever, philosopher to speak of thinking as a *pathos* – as something to be undergone or endured. On her reading, this insight is the core of the Socratic idea of philosophy as beginning in wonder. Like Heidegger, she saw that version of wonder as something deeper than the passing astonishment that arises when we first encounter something strange. She also agreed with him that what Plato had Socrates enact was something different from the kind of methodical thinking we now recognise as characterising the modern sciences. She was sceptical, nonetheless, about the implications of Heidegger's way of appropriating Socratic wonder.

Arendt comments in her essay that although surprise and astonishment at the unusual may well be the beginnings of scientific thought – and of some forms of philosophy – the kind of thinking celebrated in the *Theaetetus* relates, as Heidegger observes, not to the unusual but to the everyday: it is a response to things with which we are thoroughly acquainted and familiar. Contrary to being quietened by knowledge, this thinking that begins in wonder is a *pathos* to be endured and sustained. However, Arendt sees Heidegger as having added to this Socratic *pathos* something about which she is more cautious – the idea that, for wonder to take this form, thinkers must take it up and accept it as their 'abode'. This kind of philosophical thinking is supposed to involve retreat into a 'place of stillness', drawing what is distant into nearness. Pursuing this theme, Arendt suggests that the 'abode' of which Heidegger speaks lies, in a metaphysical sense, outside the places in which human affairs habitually take place.

Arendt sees the capacity for sustained engagement in such intense thoughtful wondering as exceptional. The propensity to wonder – at least occasionally – at the everyday may be inherent in all thinkers, and out of it each will develop traits of thought that are appropriate for them. However, the rare capacity to take up such thinking as one's 'permanent abode' is another matter. It is, she acknowledges, as an exemplar of the sustained capacity to make wondering his 'abode' that Heidegger is to be honoured. She is nonetheless troubled about the ramifications of such withdrawal.

It is an honorific essay, rather than a thoroughgoing critique of Heidegger's thought, and Arendt's remarks should be taken in that context. Yet they do resonate with her troubled evaluation of the political implications of Heidegger's withdrawal – literally as well as metaphorically – into a domain of contemplation. Her perception of his ideal of detached wonder at the usual – to the detriment of appropriate thoughtful engagement with exceptional human affairs – reflected her disappointment at Heidegger's own choices in dark times. Having been shaken by his apparent lack of judgement in relation to issues associated with the rise of Nazism, she came also to question whether his approach to philosophy was more generally indicative of a flawed capacity for politically informed judgement. Perhaps Heidegger never found his way back from that 'abode' of wonder to the political response which his times demanded.

Arendt's own thoughts on wonder are an important strand in her articulation of the ideal of 'passionate thinking' in *The Life of the Mind*, which was also published in 1971. In the section,

'What Makes Us Think?', she again discusses Plato's remarks in the *Theaetetus* about wonder, linking them with the 'wonder-struck beholding' that Homer usually reserved for those human beings to whom the gods appear. She points out that it was a peculiarity of those Greek gods that they appeared in familiar human guises, and were recognised as divinities only by those with whom they had initiated contact. The wonder they elicited was thus not something that humans could themselves summon up. That, she says, was what made this wonder a *pathos* – something to be undergone. 'In other words, what sets men wondering is something familiar and yet normally invisible, and something men are forced to *admire*.'[5]

The basis for what Arendt calls 'passionate thinking' is thus 'neither puzzlement nor surprise nor perplexity'. It is, rather, 'an *admiring* wonder'. The pause it induces in mental activity awaits a transformation into a distinctive kind of thinking, which is itself something to be 'endured'. There are some clear affinities with Heidegger in these remarks, yet there are also some important differences. The *pathos* that Arendt associates with wonder, and the thinking it generates, are far removed from the gaping stupor ridiculed by Descartes. Yet this thinking is also very different from the Heideggerian intense gaze, doggedly directed at the usual.

Arendt's version of 'admiring wonder' plays into her later discussion of the kind of mental activity involved in what she calls 'judgement'. Those reflections were intended to be the basis for the third Part of *The Life of the Mind* – to follow on from 'Thinking' and 'Willing' – which remained uncompleted at the time of her death. Arendt's insights into the connections between wonder and judgement were never fully developed, but her suggestive observations about these connections open up the possibility of a different trajectory for the revival of Socratic wonder from the one pursued by Heidegger.

In her discussion of 'admiring wonder' in *The Life of the Mind*, she notes in passing that it can be found in many variations throughout the history of modern philosophy. Unfortunately, we do not know what she may have had in mind. The only instance she offers is an intriguing reference to the 'acquiescence' implied in Spinoza's notorious remark, in the *Theological-Political Treatise*, that the more powerful dominate the less, just as big fish forever eat smaller ones. It may seem an odd illustration for the idea of possible variations on Socratic wonder. Yet the reference evokes the spirit of ironic detachment with which Spinoza contemplates the 'necessity' enacted in the operations of political power. This is a different form of detachment, both from the gaping stupor criticised by Descartes, and from the demanding intensity of Heideggerian withdrawal. On the account that Arendt was able to do no more than sketch, it yields the idea of an engaged thinking whose proper expression is, not moral acceptance or approval, but rather a striving for clarity of judgement in the midst of acknowledged uncertainty.

There are echoes in Arendt's treatment of wonder of her earlier controversial analysis, in *Eichmann in Jerusalem*, of what came to be known as 'the banality of evil'. She saw Eichmann's form of obedience as an acceptance of ready-made conclusions, to the detriment of active thought. She argued that his self-defence displayed an inanity that could not be captured in an alleged failure of logic. It reflected, rather, a distinctive and horrifying form of 'unthinking'. The capacity for wonder was for Arendt closely connected with the capacity for engaged, responsible thinking of the kind that Eichmann so manifestly lacked. She reflected on the political dimensions of these interrelated capacities in a passage in Part One of *The Life of the Mind*, which points towards the envisaged, but never realised, third Part:

> When everybody is swept away unthinkingly by what everyone else does and believes in, those who think are drawn out of hiding because their refusal to join in is conspicuous and thereby becomes a kind of action. In such emergencies, it turns out that the purging component of thinking (Socrates' midwifery, which brings out the implications of unexamined opinions and thereby destroys them – values, doctrines, theories, and even convictions) is political by implication. For this destruction has a liberating effect on another faculty, the faculty of judgement, which one may call with some reason the most political of man's mental abilities. (p. 192)

The 'engaged thinking' that Arendt reconstructed out of Socratic wonder was for her 'political by implication'. Later, in her *Lectures on Kant's Political Philosophy*, she developed the idea that the form of aesthetic judgement which Kant analysed in the *Critique of Judgement* had implications for a more general understanding of the political aspects of judgement. She argued that, just as what Kant and his contemporaries called 'judgements of taste' were not an expression of individual caprice, so too the critiques made by 'judging spectators' of their own and others' actions were objectively based evaluations, expressing a shared community of judgement.

For her, such judgements are expressions of human sociability; they are grounded in ways of being together. She talks in the lectures of the role played in the *Critique of Judgement* by an ideal of 'enlargement of the mind', attained by comparing our judgements with possible rather than actual judgements of others. We develop that capacity by putting ourselves imaginatively in the place of others – training the imagination to 'go visiting'.[6]

Although these ideas were never fully developed, they allow us to see the political orientation that Arendt wanted to give to a reconstructed Socratic wonder. Withdrawal in order to judge action – especially the past collective action of a group, which becomes visible in memory and through history – emerges here as very different, both in method and in spirit, from what made Arendt uneasy about Heidegger's talk of the 'abode' of wondering thought. Rather than an onerously cultivated pursuit of a distinctively philosophical cast of mind, this reconstructed version of Socratic wonder becomes something readily accessible, and necessary for collective political consciousness.

There is a temporal aspect to Arendt's version of judgement, which connects its 'objectivity' to its political character. On the account of it she has sketched, we put ourselves in imagination at a position in the future from which our own actions can be judged. The 'objectivity' does not arise from deferral to the judgements of actual others - whether present or future – which might be seen as conferring authority or legitimacy. The benchmarks against which our actions are to be considered are not actual but possible judgements, taken into account in our imagining. There are echoes here of the elusive 'standard of taste' which figured in eighteenth-century debates on the objectivity of aesthetic evaluation – the idea of a shared response which made such judgements 'communicable', rather than merely subjective.

Arendt's crucial insight into the kind of objectivity involved in the faculty of judgement is that it is not a matter of an agreed consensus in actual judgement. This objectivity involves, rather, bringing the imagination into the very heart of judgement. In 'going visiting', imagination draws in other possible judgers. It is this exercise of imagination that makes judgement 'sociable' – or, in a broad sense, 'political' – by nature. On her account, the 'engaged thinking' associated with Socratic wonder – rather than involving a withdrawal from the political – draws us into the collective, sociable aspects of imagining.

In Chapter 8, we will see how Arendt's relatively undeveloped thoughts on wonder's connections with judgement might be brought to bear on ideas of social critique in a contemporary context. However, there is also another path through which contemporary philosophy has tried to reconnect with Socratic themes related to wonder: Jacques Derrida's concern with the interrelated notions of *aporia* and *singularity*. This too is relevant for understanding contemporary strategies of social critique.

Notes

1 Martin Heidegger, *The Fundamental Concepts of Metaphysics*: *World, Finitude, Solitude*, trans. William McNeill and Nicholas Walker (Bloomington and Minneapolis: Indiana University Press, 1995), pp. 59–68. Further page references will be given in the main text.
2 Martin Heidegger, *Basic Questions of Philosophy: Select 'Problems' of 'Logic'*, trans. Richard Rojcewicz and André Schuwer (Bloomington and Indianapolis: Indiana University Press, 1994), p. 4. Further page references will be given in the main text.
3 Ludwig Wittgenstein, *Lecture on Ethics*, ed. Edoardo Zamuner, Emmelinda Valentina Di Lascio and D. K. Levy (Oxford: John Wiley and Sons, 2014), pp. 47–8.
4 Hannah Arendt, 'Martin Heidegger at Eighty', *New York Review of Books*, 21 October 1971.
5 Hannah Arendt, *The Life of the Mind* (New York and London: Harcourt Brace Jovanovich, 1971), p. 143.
6 Hannah Arendt, *Lectures on Kant's Political Philosophy*, ed. Ronald Beiner (Chicago: University of Chicago Press, 1982), p. 43. I discuss Arendt's treatment of Kant's political essays more fully in *Enlightenment Shadows* (Oxford: Oxford University Press, 2013), Ch. 7.

7

Derrida on *Aporia*, Time and Mortality

Jacques Derrida rarely talked explicitly of wonder. Yet he had a deep interest in issues arising from the ancient idea of *aporia* – the ancient, and to us now familiar, notion of the condition in which a perplexed mind comes to a halt with no clear path to follow. His explorations of that condition are imbued with the philosophical history of wonder. In a set of lectures published in 1992 as the volume *Aporias*, he offered a 'revitalised' version of what he described as the 'old, worn-out Greek term'.[1]

Derrida on Singularity

Central to Derrida's reconstruction of *aporia* is an emphasis on a term we have already encountered in relation to Spinoza's treatment of wonder – *singularity*. What is fascinating in the experience of *aporia*, Derrida says, is that we are 'singularly exposed in our absolute and absolutely naked uniqueness, that is to say, disarmed, delivered to the other, incapable even of sheltering ourselves behind what could still protect the interiority of a secret'.[2] It is a striking – and at first sight perplexing – elaboration of the ancient idea of *aporia*. How does the idea of a blocked path, allowing nowhere to go, yield our own 'naked uniqueness' or 'deliverance to the other'? How did 'otherness' get into the picture? The trajectory of thought that brings Derrida to this point becomes clearer in his discussion of *aporia* in his *Memoires for Paul de Man*. Talking there of de Man's frequent appeals to the notion of *aporia* in his late texts, he has this to say:

> I believe that we would misunderstand it if we tried to hold it to its most literal meaning: an absence of path, a paralysis before roadblocks, the immobilisation of thinking, the impossibility of advancing, a barrier blocking the future. On the contrary, it seems to me that the experience of the aporia, such as de Man deciphers it, gives or promises the thinking of the path, provokes the thinking of the very possibility of what still remains unthinkable or unthought, indeed impossible. The figures of rationality are profiled and outlined in the madness of the aporetic.[3]

Following de Man on this point, Derrida treats *aporia* as something more than the mere absence of a path forward for thought. There is an important shift of emphasis here, though it is not inconsistent with the ancient Greek idea. For Derrida, this intellectual hiatus – the mind's loss of movement – is to be taken, not as an incipient paralysis, but rather as a constructive pause in its ongoing activity. In this respect, Derrida's treatment of *aporia* is similar to Spinoza's treatment of wonder; but there is no surrounding metaphysical framework – no theory of mind as *conatus* – to explain the renewal of activity. Nor is there any Cartesian effort of will to bring a remedy for gaping stupor – no bland idea of a resolute moving forward. Derrida cautions, ironically: 'When someone suggests to you a solution for escaping an impasse, you can be almost sure that he is ceasing to understand, assuming that he had understood anything up to that point.'[4]

That wry remark could be heard as an expression of irritation with something that has become a trite commonplace in contemporary discourse. 'Moving forward' is often invoked as a supposedly positive response to a set-back or catastrophe – not infrequently to the exasperation of those directly experiencing the trauma. However, Derrida's remark has a deeper import than the mere repudiation of a cliché. There are some echoes here of Heidegger's call for staying in the intellectual space opened up by wonder. Like Heidegger, and like Arendt, Derrida is criticising the impulse to bring to a precipitate end the state of reflection induced by *aporia*. However, he is putting his own stamp on that creative pause for thought. To see what is distinctive in it, it is again helpful to go back to Spinoza's rejection of Descartes' treatment of wonder. The connections are there to be made, though Derrida does not himself make them.

Singularity remains, in contemporary philosophical discussion, a shifting and often perplexing notion. It can be found in many debates influenced by, or responding to, Nietzsche – whose talk of 'eternal return of the same' had already engaged its paradoxes of being and becoming – as well as to Heidegger.[5] It is not always easy to keep a grip on it. Looking at the affinities – and the differences – between Derrida's use of singularity and the ways in which Spinoza talked of it can help to anchor the term. For Spinoza, singularity was a feature of an unfamiliar object confronting the mind intent on knowledge. Struck by the apparent uniqueness of what is before us, our thought initially finds nowhere to go. The hiatus is in the activity of thinking, yet the singularity resides in the object. It is not the mind or its thinking that is properly said to be *singular*; rather, it is the thing apprehended. For Derrida, in contrast, singularity seems to be applied, not only to the object, but also to the mind's experience in apprehending it – and to the mind itself. Yet there is a trajectory of thought here – a 'path', perhaps – which can take us from Spinoza on wonder to Derrida on *aporia*.

If what is before us is such that our thinking cannot get any purchase on it at all, then that is to say that this thing confronting us is utterly 'other'. Thus, the experience of *aporia* can be said to deliver us to the otherness of the object. This otherness is, however, double-edged. With nowhere for thinking to go, we are thrown back on ourselves. So there is here a reciprocal otherness: the thinking self is utterly other to what is before it. There is a lack of common ground – not only between things we are trying to think about, but also between us and those objects of thought. What is before us cannot be assimilated – either *to* other things or *by* the knowing subject. *Aporia* can thus be seen as a state of incipient alienation. This sense of double-edged otherness, which is a feature of Derrida's 'revitalisation' of *aporia*, is discernible especially in his late seminars, where he reflects on the idea of singularity in relation to political aspects of sovereignty, to its enactment in the death penalty, and to death itself.

In the first volume of Derrida's seminars on *The Beast and the Sovereign*, the notion of singularity is associated with the theme of 'exceptionalism' – with the paradoxes in a Sovereign's power to make, but also to suspend, law. That power gives a Sovereign 'the exceptional right to place oneself above right'. Singularity is here the source of the instability in the conceptual triad: *beast, human, divine*. It underlies 'the risks carrying the human sovereign above the human, towards divine omnipotence'. It is what can make the Sovereign 'look like the most brutal beast, who respects nothing, scorns the law, situates himself above the law, at a distance from the law'. It is thus the basis of the troubling resemblance – the 'obscure and fascinating complicity' – between sovereignty, animality and criminality.[6]

The seminars explore that 'complicity' from a starting point in the mantra which runs through La Fontaine's fable, 'The Lamb and the Wolf': that the reason of the stronger is always the best. There is a deliberate ambiguity in the mantra. The 'reason of the stronger', which is said to be the best, might be taken either as the reason that in fact prevails or as the reason that *ought* to prevail – by right, and according to justice. The ironic observation conveyed by the ambiguity is of course that the greater strength of 'the stronger' is perhaps not incidental to its being 'the best'. The predicament of Fontaine's lamb is not unlike that of Spinoza's small, powerless fish confronting 'sovereign natural right'.

The subtle shifts in thought that Derrida tracks between *sovereign*, *beast* and *criminal* are pervaded by the sense of wonder. They are evocatively described in terms reminiscent of Plato's *Theaetetus*. Derrida talks of a 'vertigo of the mind', of the bottomless 'abyss', of 'what can make your head swim'. The resemblance to Plato's descriptions of the experience of wonder is not incidental. The mind-stopping singularity inherent in the idea of sovereignty draws us into a chase of interconnected meanings, which put the mind into giddying motion. It is dazzling verbal play – with serious conceptual intent. As Derrida said of de Man's *aporias*, the hiatus induced by the experience of *aporia*, rather than bringing intellectual paralysis, delivers us to the depths of the concept under investigation. It provokes the thinking of what had previously seemed impossible to think.

Derrida's selection of the idea of 'sovereignty' for this style of analysis is of course itself an exercise in semantic dexterity. Here the singularity is implicit in what we already understand of the meaning of 'sovereignty', otherwise the conceptual chase could not begin. Yet the path which seems visible at the start quickly turns out to be an illusion. It is true that we are led to a deeper understanding of sovereignty, but we have not been taken where we thought we were going – not into a reiteration of sovereign transcendence of law, but into the darker side of its implicit exceptionalism.

The dark twists are even more apparent in Derrida's manoeuvres with the notion of singularity in his discussions of time and mortality, which unfold in the second volume of *The Beast and the Sovereign*. Here, the unthinkability of the singular is at its starkest – in relation to the thought of death. We have already seen connections between *aporia* and mortality in Plato's Dialogues: Socratic *aporia* was powerfully induced by the impossibility of knowing what, if anything, lies beyond death. There are, of course, also resonances in Derrida's discussion of Heidegger's reflections on the lived experience of time and mortality.

Time and Mortality

The perplexity of *aporia* takes on another dimension in Derrida's elaboration of it in terms of singularity. In his 'revitalisation' of *aporia* – which finds singularity in the mind's sense of itself, as well as in the object it confronts in wonder – the disorientation goes beyond the paralysis of inquiry. The mind is shaken in its sense of what it is, rather than just in its capacity to know other things. This aspect of Derrida's version of *aporia* emerges especially in his discussion of 'world' and 'solitude', where the Heideggerian overtones become more explicit. It leads into a powerful dramatisation of the confrontation with singularity in Derrida's reading of Defoe's famous description of Robinson Crusoe's shocked encounter with a single footprint in the sand.[7]

Crusoe is initially paralysed by the sight of the footprint – as though he had been struck by lightning or thunder. He is astonished by the apparent evidence of another human presence on 'his' island. That consternation is overtaken by an even more disturbing thought. The print becomes more uncanny for being 'possibly his own, on a path already trodden'. Temporal disorientation now joins the lack of spatial bearings which had afflicted Crusoe in the early days of his isolation. It is, Derrida tells us, as if he were living his own past as a terrifying future, which comes to be thought as the coming again of something already past. This temporal dislocation passes over into a fear of death:

> He believes he is shortly going to die, that he is running after his death or that death is running after him, that life will have been so short, and thus, as though he were already dead, because of this race with his revenance, everything that happens to him happens not as something new, fresh, or to come, but as . . . already past, already seen, to come as yesterday and not as tomorrow. (p. 50)

These are tortuous passages. As in other reflections of Derrida's on time and futurity, on mortality and grief, he plays here with suspending the ordinary laws of tense logic. That manoeuvre brings on yet another form of wonder-induced vertigo: 'As I run to death always after yesterday, yesterday will always be to come: not tomorrow, in the future, but to come, ahead, there in front, the day before yesterday' (p. 54). If this be play, it has nonetheless a profound seriousness. It exposes the deeper 'logic' of emotions involved in grief and mourning – whether for others or for oneself: 'I am no longer present, I am already yesterday, I enjoy from yesterday, . . . because only yesterday will have given me, only my death or the feeling of my death, a death that will have taken me by speed, only my death lets me enjoy and take pleasure – in this very moment' (p. 52). The sequence of thought is complex, the expression deliberately breathless. Yet there is also a tenacious conceptual rigour in this exercise.

Maurice Blanchot, in *Writing the Disaster* – from which Derrida quotes in these passages on time and mortality – engages in similar mind-bending verbal play. He speaks there of dying as the imminence of what has already come to pass. He talks also of 'the disaster of a time without present which we endure by waiting, by awaiting a misfortune which is not still to come, but which has always already come upon us and which cannot be present.' In this sense, he says, the future and the past come to the same 'since both are without present'.[8] There is a similar discussion in Blanchot's *The Instant of My Death* – a short, powerful narrative about a young man's reprieve from a firing squad during the Second World War. In an extended essay on that piece, Derrida talks of Blanchot's temporal manoeuvres as involving 'an *unbelievable* tense', which 'seems to deport what has always, from all time, already taken place toward the coming of the to-come'.[9]

It can all sound like mesmerising linguistic gymnastics. Yet these strange but luminous discussions resonate with the philosophical history of wonder: the strange, volatile mix of intense emotions; the shifts between immobilisation and restless vacillation; the struggle to understand what seems inherently impossible to think. Able to take place only once, our deaths seem to represent ultimate singularity – and hence ultimate unthinkability. In the lack of anything in common with our understanding of other things we have experienced, death cannot be thought. Yet, as Blanchot says, although it is 'unshareable', it is nonetheless something we have in common with all.[10] It is a mark of this paradoxical singularity of death, in the midst of its being common to all, that it is something at which we are individually inexperienced – no matter how often we may observe it happening to others.

His earlier remarks on time and mortality in *Memoires for Paul de Man* help clarify some of the moves Derrida makes in later treatments of the theme. In his reflections there on death, grief and bereaved friendship, he stresses the significance of the future in temporal consciousness. The point relates to another aspect of singularity: the future makes determinate what happens in the present. The 'absolutely unforeseeable', he says, is always the condition of any event. 'Even when it seems to go back to a buried past, what comes about always comes from the future.'[11] The content of what happens now – what it is – depends on what is still future; it is 'determinate' only from a perspective not yet available.

Derrida also pursues the theme of singularity, in relation to 'otherness' and death, in a reading of Kierkegaard's passages on Abraham's 'fear and trembling', which we have seen discussed by Agacinski. Here too Derrida connects singularity with reflections on temporality:

> We tremble in the strange repetition that ties an irrefutable past (a shock has been felt, some trauma has already affected us) to a future that cannot be anticipated; anticipated but unpredictable; *apprehended*, yet, and this is why there is a future, apprehended precisely *as* unforeseeable, unpredictable; approached *as* unapproachable.[12]

In Derrida's reading of the Kierkegaard passages, the theme of the 'otherness' of singularity is developed especially in relation to the 'absolute singularity' of Abraham's God. He goes on, however, to extend it to every encounter with an other. *Tout autre est tout autre.* 'Every other (one) is every (bit) other.'[13]

There is something deeply paradoxical in the idea of the *singular* that has emerged in these reflections of Derrida on time and mortality – a determinacy which depends on a perspective in principle unavailable; an irremediable singularity, which is nonetheless common to all. We may seem to have come a long way from Spinoza's treatment of singularity, with its reassuring affirmation of the mind's continued efforts to understand in the face of apparent unthinkability. Yet there are echoes here of Spinoza's tantalising observation in Part V of the *Ethics* – often quoted, but little understood – that the wise think of death least of all things, and that their wisdom is a meditation, not on death, but on life. Reading Derrida and Spinoza together suggests, perhaps, that the reason Spinoza's wise do not think of death is that they are wise enough to recognise its unthinkability.

Wonder and Collective Stupidity

In his seminars on *The Beast and the Sovereign*, Derrida does not directly address the nature of wonder or its role in the life of the mind. However, he does offer an extended treatment of the closely related – though at first sight antithetical – notion of stupidity, which we have already seen in Flaubert. The connotations of *bêtise* as something akin to animality make it relevant to Derrida's concern with the conceptual triad: *sovereign, beast, criminal*. He draws on passages in Gilles Deleuze's *Difference and Repetition* that reflect on the strangeness of the fact that *bêtise* is not, as the name might suggest, a characteristic of animals. It is rather, as Deleuze observes, 'a specifically human form of bestiality'.[14]

Deleuze argues that this *bêtise* cannot be explained by appeal to the concept of error. Rather than being a trait of particular characters or societies that have gone astray, it belongs with conditions which are 'structures of thought as such'. Flaubert's novels, he remarks, belong among the best of literary works which were 'haunted by the problem of stupidity', carrying it as far as 'the entrance to philosophy itself'. Echoing Kant's sense of a 'transcendental' inquiry as one that investigates the conditions under which something is possible, Deleuze goes on to suggest that philosophy could have – though it has not – made it the object of a 'properly transcendental question': how is stupidity, as distinct from error, possible?[15] It is a strange question, which takes Deleuze into a consideration of individuation and selfhood – into the 'terror and attraction' excited by an individual mind's contemplation of itself.

Derrida is intrigued by those resonances between Deleuze's remarks on stupidity and older philosophical reflections on the nature of human thought. He begins his discussion of *bêtise* by continuing Deleuze's reflections on the apparent strangeness of the fact that the term does not apply to animals – that, if this is indeed a form of animality, it is yet one that can be properly attributed only to humans. Echoing a famous remark of Descartes' in the *Discourse on Method*, Derrida observes ironically that *bêtise* is something which is proper to man. Like what Descartes calls 'good sense', it is the most equally distributed trait in the world – among humans.[16]

It becomes clearer that the consideration of this form of stupidity takes us into the territory of wonder when

Derrida – prompted by Deleuze's references to Flaubert's *Bouvard and Pecuchet* – moves on to 'follow the track of Flaubert', whom he describes as 'an obligatory reference on stupidity' (p. 157). Derrida here pushes further Deleuze's observation that a predisposition to *bêtise* is integral to 'the structures of thought as such'. With some relish, he develops the point mischievously in relation to the kind of thinking involved in philosophy. He facetiously suggests that this form of stupidity is inherent in the philosopher's desire to reach conclusions about the natures of things – including the nature of stupidity itself. The upshot of his argument is that where there is wonder – the supposed beginnings of philosophy – there too lurks a susceptibility to the form of stupidity identified with *bêtise*. Moreover, in so far as philosophers seek to understand *bêtise* – a pervasive phenomenon of thought itself – they themselves fall into that condition.

Provocative – and potentially outrageous – though all that may sound, engaging with it can illuminate wonder's relations with the fundamental activity of human thinking. Beneath the teasing lies a serious point: wonder and *bêtise* belong together. They shadow one another – at times mocking one another, by changing places – in the mind's efforts to understand. Let us then follow Derrida a little further back down that 'track of Flaubert'. He is drawn to Flaubert's letter from Egypt which, as we have seen, impressed Sartre with its metaphors of solidity. The foolish Thompson's enactment of monumental stupidity – etched in stone by his folly in carving his name on the edifice – becomes for Derrida an emblem of the philosopher's desire for definitive conclusions. The style of thinking epitomised in philosophy is presented by Derrida as itself a paradigm of Flaubert's equation of stupidity with 'wanting to reach conclusions'.

Derrida, however, takes Flaubert's derision about that desire for conclusions further. For him, there can be a kind of stupidity, not just in wanting conclusions to the philosopher's question, but in the determination to ask them in the first place. There can, he says, be a strange and troubling affinity between *bêtise* and a certain obstinacy in asking – or asking oneself – questions. 'There is without doubt a *bêtise* of the question, as there is of affirmation, as there is of negation' (p. 306). There at the very place where philosophy is supposed to begin, lurks a kind of stupidity; and it is precisely in trying to 'reach a conclusion' that the philosopher is most prone to this stupidity.

Derrida's point – at the expense of philosophers – is that not all prolonged asking of questions is a manifestation of constructive intellectual activity. The rigidity of thought which is the mark of *bêtise* – the closing of minds – can find expression in the stubborn persistence in asking questions, as well as in dogmatically held opinion. From the stupor of wonder, with which philosophy supposedly begins, we can readily pass into *bêtise*, and philosophy can be complicit in that stupidity. Indeed it can be at play in the very effort to bring philosophical understanding to the topic of stupidity itself. In struggling to understand *bêtise*, Derrida says, we 'engender *bêtise* in the very gaze, in the sustained attention, study, or reflection, claiming to know its essence and its meaning' (p. 158). To assume that there is an essence of *bêtise*, awaiting the philosopher's definition, may be itself already a sign of *bêtise*.

Some of this can pass as playful teasing at the expense of the pretensions of philosophers. Yet there is also a serious point at stake. The common posture of the philosopher's effort to understand – to come to a conclusion – can be complicit in a form of stupidity. We may well hear echoes there of Descartes' warning that the halt in mental activity induced by wonder can readily turn into a more prolonged mental paralysis. Intellect can be deadened by dogged questioning, as well as by gaping stupor. However, Derrida makes an additional point, which he has developed out of Flaubert's treatment of the deadening effects of 'received ideas'. It is possible, Derrida warns, to have a 'mimeticism' – something akin to a 'contagion' of *bêtise*. Indeed, this form of stupidity is characteristically a collective matter: 'One is never *bête* all on one's own and by oneself' (p. 158).

The central point here has some affinities with Sartre's emphasis on the intersubjectivity of authentic thinking, though Derrida credits Flaubert with the insight, rather than unfairly projecting *bêtise* onto him. The circulation of stale opinion – the solidity of received 'conclusions' – can stifle the life of the mind. The oppressive force of collective stupidities can – as Bouvard and Pecuchet came piteously to see – make outcasts of those who wonder.[17] Fortunately, wonder can also become itself a force for reckoning with the collective closing of minds. In the next chapter we will explore some of the political implications of wonder in the face of collective stupidity.

Notes

1 Jacques Derrida, *Aporias*, trans. Thomas Dutot (Stanford: Stanford University Press, 1993), p. 12.
2 Derrida, *Aporias*, p. 12.
3 Jacques Derrida, *Memoires for Paul de Man* (revised edition), trans. Cecile Lindsay, Jonathan Culler, Eduardo Cadava and Peggy Kamuf (New York: Columbia University Press, 1989), p. 132.
4 Derrida, *Aporias*, p. 32.
5 Heidegger's brief commentary on Nietzsche's 'eternal return of the same', written in 1939, is included in Martin Heidegger, *Nietzsche*, Vol. III, ed.

David Farrell Krell, trans. Joan Stambaugh, David Farrell Krell and Frank A. Capuzzi (San Francisco: Harper Collins, 1991), pp. 209–15.
6. Jacques Derrida, *The Beast and the Sovereign*, Vol. I, ed. Geoffrey Bennington and Peggy Kamuf (Chicago: University of Chicago Press, 2009), p. 16.
7. Jacques Derrida, *The Beast and the Sovereign*, Vol. II, ed. Michael Lisse, Marie-Louise Mallet and Ginette Michaud, trans. Geoffrey Bennington (Chicago: University of Chicago Press, 2011), pp. 45–54.
8. Maurice Blanchot, *The Writing of the Disaster*, trans. Ann Smock (Lincoln and London: University of Nebraska Press, 1995), p. 21.
9. Maurice Blanchot, *The Instant of My Death*, with Jacques Derrida, *Demeure: Fiction and Testimony*, trans. Elizabeth Rottenberg (Stanford: Stanford University Press, 2000), p. 49.
10. Blanchot, *The Writing of the Disaster*, p. 23.
11. Derrida, *Memoires for Paul de Man*, p. 160.
12. Jacques Derrida, *The Gift of Death* (second edition) and *Literature in Secret*, trans. David Wills (Chicago and London: University of Chicago Press, 2008), p. 55.
13. Derrida, *Gift of Death*, p. 82.
14. Gilles Deleuze, *Difference and Repetition*, trans. Paul Patton (New York: Columbia University Press, 1994), p. 150.
15. Deleuze, *Difference and Repetition*, pp. 150–3.
16. Derrida, *Beast and Sovereign*, Vol. I, p. 138. Further page references will be given in the main text.
17. Derrida elaborates on the significance of Flaubert's insights into stupidity in a discussion of Spinoza's influence on his artistic theory and practice, in an essay 'An Idea of Flaubert: "Plato's Letter"', in *Psyche: Invention of the Other*, Vol. I, ed. Peggy Kamuf and Elizabeth Rottenberg (Stanford: Stanford University Press, 2007), pp. 299-317.

8

Political Wonder and Social Critique

Sartre complained of the lack of organisation in Flaubert's putative Dictionary. There was, he thought, no common thread in its disparate mix of puns, word-plays, metaphors and misjudged opinions. We can perhaps see more clearly now than Sartre could have the significance of Flaubert's passion for collecting stupidities. What his 'received ideas' have in common is that they have all been said before – repeatedly. They are clichés that circulate among social groups, serving to legitimate uncritical opinion. However, Flaubert's admittedly chaotic collection of oft-repeated phrases reveals more than the deleterious effects of repetition on effective communication. His intended juxtaposition of the Dictionary with the pathos of the adventures and misfortunes of Bouvard and Pecuchet gives to his lists a depth and satirical force which might not otherwise be apparent. They illuminate the oppressive power of the cliché to reinforce prejudice and to mask collective failure in the exercise of judgement.

Under contemporary conditions of global communication, the political effects of such constantly repeated slogans, mantras and sense-bestowing narratives are more apparent. Resort to what Flaubert called 'received ideas' can indicate wilful obfuscation for political ends, no less than it can signal a disregard for the rich resources of language to add vitality to expression. The apparently thoughtless cliché can conceal a calculated strategy for disguise or distortion. Flaubert's Dictionary does not belong only to a tradition of French satire. It can also claim a place in a less easily categorised tradition of demystification of rhetoric. It contains the seeds of the kind of exercise to which George Orwell gave prominence in his famous critiques of political language.

Political Language and Social Imaginaries

Edmund Burke had already called attention to the political effects of language when, in his *Philosophical Enquiry into the Sublime and Beautiful*, he stressed the power of words to intensify emotion through the evocation of images, acting largely unmediated through reason. When that power is understood, it can also be exploited in the opposite direction – in the deliberate choice of phrases which desensitise the power of imagery. It was Orwell's achievement to expose those desensitising strategies, of which he offered some striking – and still relevant – illustrations in his 1946 essay, 'Politics and the English Language':

> Defenceless villages are bombarded from the air, the inhabitants are driven out into the countryside, the cattle machine-gunned, the huts set on fire with incendiary bullets: this is called *pacification*. Millions of peasants are robbed of their farms and seen trudging along the roads with no more than they can carry: this is called *transfer of population* or *rectification of frontiers*. People are imprisoned for years without trial, or shot in the back of the head or sent to die of scurvy in Arctic lumber camps: this

is called *elimination of unreliable elements*. Such phraseology is needed if one wants to name things without calling up mental pictures of them.[1]

Politically motivated redescription can work either to intensify emotion or to neutralise it. Insight into the ways in which the emotive force of imagery can be manipulated and exploited has been an important strand in more recent strategies for demystifying political language. Derrida's elaboration of Flaubert's insights on stupidity opens up possibilities for developing strategies to expose current exercises in desensitisation and obfuscation.

On Derrida's reading of La Fontaine's ironic fable of the lion and the lamb, it is inevitable that the 'reason of the strongest' always prevails. So, too, it can seem that the scales are loaded in favour of the 'contagion' of politically inspired clichés. Yet there is a note of optimism in Derrida's attempts to revive the political power of old Socratic ideas of *aporia*. Plato had Socrates relate his skills in inducing the experience of *aporia* to the social significance of the kind of thinking that was supposed to 'begin in wonder'. In their modern versions, also, experiences of wonder-inducing *aporia* can be a stimulus to revitalising social critique.

The Socratic ideal of the philosophical thinker as gadfly has inspired many social critics. Yet its content has remained nebulous throughout later philosophical commentary. The practice of Socratic questioning may be invoked in rhetoric about the social relevance of philosophy, but there is little guidance as to what a contemporary philosophical gadfly might actually do. What can the subsequent philosophical history of wonder teach us about its bearing on contemporary social critique?

We have seen Spinoza, and later Derrida, show how spurious certainties can debilitate the life of the mind. The frequently repeated narratives that bind a group together can also come to restrict an individual mind's freedom to move. They can become a source of intellectual paralysis. When we acquiesce in that hardening of thought, we put ourselves at the mercy of what Flaubert called 'received ideas'. Yet when we find ourselves wondering at the operations and outcomes of that collective stupidity, that can itself be the beginnings of a rejuvenated capacity for collective judgement.

Spinoza's concern was with the inhibiting effects of the misuse of biblical stories – and the wonders, miracles and prophecies they narrated – on the acceptance of rigorous procedures for scientific inquiry. However, his treatment of the imagination, and of its interactions with emotion, has broader implications for the critique of socially embedded fictions. His exposure of the interrelations of imagination and emotion in the *Ethics*, and especially in his political writings, highlight the collective dimensions of imagining. There are some affinities here between Spinoza's criticisms of the theologians' misuse of social narratives and more recent critiques of 'social imaginaries' – the unexamined assumptions and recurring imagery that become embedded in social practices and institutional structures.

The idea of a 'social imaginary' as a tool of social critique is meant to evoke a network of attitudes, assumptions and emotions which shapes patterns of thinking – usually in ways that go unrecognised. Cornelius Castoriadis drew on psychoanalytic theory to offer a description of this 'context-related' form of imagining as something more than a faculty operating in individual minds. For him, such an 'imaginary' is a collectively generated phenomenon, in which individuals find themselves immersed.[2] More recently, Charles Taylor has elaborated the idea as involving a sense of a social group's 'whole predicament' – of how they stand to each other, how they got where they are, how they are related to other groups. Because of the unlimited and indefinite nature of that notion, it cannot be adequately expressed through explicit doctrines. This lack of clear limits, Taylor suggests, is a reason for speaking of it as an 'imaginary' rather than as a theory.[3]

The idea of an 'imaginary' is itself a concept with shifting – and sometimes confusing – content. It can be a psychoanalytic construct, evoking ideas of the unconscious. 'Social imaginaries' can be clusters of images; they can also be construed as unspoken, inexplicit beliefs or assumptions. What is important for my purposes here is the idea of a form of collective imagining, which shapes individual thought processes. The political import of insight into the operations of such contextualised imagining has been brought out persuasively by Chiara Bottici in her book *Imaginal Politics*.[4] For Bottici, what is in the relevant sense 'imaginary' is not a collection of inner states possessed by individuals. Nor is it produced by a faculty whose function is to summon up what is not real. It is rather a domain – a context – that is more appropriately described as 'possessing us'.

The concept that Bottici here calls the 'imaginal' – as distinct from old senses of the 'imaginary' – is crafted to encompass products both of imagination, as an individual faculty, and of the broader context of collective imagining, as well as a complex interaction between the two. If we want to engage with the political aspects of imagination, she argues, it is inadequate to think of imagination as simply a faculty that represents what does not exist – the unreal. That would imply that the imagination is relevant only to aesthetic or utopian domains, rather than to the political dimensions of human life. She insists that we need to address here, not only unreal products of imagining, but also how we collectively imagine the contexts in which our thinking occurs.

This approach to the imaginary attempts to address the contemporary realities of a proliferation of images, as well as a constant bombardment of verbal messages. What does this have to do with wonder? Given the historical connections between the philosophical understanding of wonder and theories of the imagination, it is not surprising that we should find some parallel developments. Bottici's extension of the 'imaginary' beyond the domains of aesthetic appreciation, and utopian or dystopian fiction, resembles in some ways Heidegger's efforts to reconnect with ancient ideas of wondering *at* what is real. However, like Arendt, Bottici treats the implications of such an extension as being strongly political. Her expansion of the imaginary to include the real along with the unreal has implications for how an exercise like Flaubert's exposure of collective 'stupidities' might be brought to bear on social critique in a contemporary context.

Sartre, as we saw, constructed his 'Flaubert' figure as a simulacrum of the stupidity which the real Flaubert loathed – as if he were himself at the mercy of the stale clichés he collected. Flaubert became for Sartre the enactment of a consciousness unable to transcend the deadening repetition of trite formulae. His lists of received opinions reflected passivity and inertia – the density of imposed response. For Sartre, those lists represented a stupidity that is 'infinite', because it always 'comes from elsewhere – from another time and place'. It is, he thought, a stupidity that is 'inert and opaque, imposed by its own weight', with laws that cannot be modified. Stupidity of that kind, he suggested, is 'a *thing*, finally because it possesses the impassability and impenetrability of natural facts'.[5]

Yet the real Flaubert, as Sartre himself at times acknowledged, was an attentive, critical individual consciousness, highly attuned to the prevailing stupidity of his times – enduring it, but also actively exposing it. Sartre's talk of taking individuals as typifying what was universal in their times was meant to justify what seems a crude projection onto the individual Flaubert of the very condition he was trying to expose. Yet it was an exercise which did point towards more subtle strategies for articulating the distinctive collective mentalities within which individuals think.

Having in mind more recent developments in the understanding of 'social imaginaries', we can now articulate more clearly just how a revitalised sensitivity to the experience of wonder might become a powerful source of social critique. What are our contemporary versions of 'received ideas'? And how might a modern-day Flaubert – attuned to the realities of a contextualised 'imaginary' – respond to their mind-numbing impact?

Flaubert's own insight into what he called 'stupidity' was that 'received ideas' which pass for certainties – for 'conclusions' already reached – come to act as an oppressive force, debilitating the capacity for active thinking. Yet to have that insight is already to begin to see how that force might be resisted. Insight into the circulation of such ossified remnants of active thought can also become a source of a constructive reimagining. The congealed thought of received ideas renders us passive; but coming to an understanding of that condition can bring renewed mental activity. The process can be seen as a re-enactment of Spinoza's analysis of the structure of wonder: the mind's awareness of having been brought to a halt becomes of itself a stimulus to continued activity.

Bottici's *Imaginal Politics* puts her expanded version of social imaginaries to work in analyses of the ways in which some familiar social narratives can take on the character of 'political myths'. A 'political myth', in this sense, is a narrative that responds to a collective need for significance. To take on that status, it must be a shared response to the political conditions and experiences of a social group. Such sustaining myths have what Bottici describes as 'condensational power': they can be distilled into a few pages – a few phrases or icons. The circulation of such 'myths' can have a political charge which resists clear analysis. They can profoundly influence our most fundamental perceptions of the world, while their very vagueness allows them to elude scrutiny.

The idea of a 'clash of civilisations' between Islam and 'the West' is for Bottici a notable example of such a political myth. Proposed as a thesis – especially by Samuel Huntington in his 1996 book, *The Clash of Civilisations and the Remaking of the World Order* – it had been largely repudiated as too simplistic to capture the political complexities of the time. But after the terrorist attacks in New York of September 2001, and others in Europe, the idea of such a clash became a widespread and powerful motif, responding to a need to make sense of current events.

A notion which proves inadequate at the level of theory can thus function nonetheless as a successful 'political myth'. It can answer to a need for readily accessible meaning, and it can be strengthened by association with other similar constructs: on Bottici's account, this is what has happened with the relation between 'the clash of civilisations' and the 'war on terror'. People can act and talk *as if* a clash between civilisations were taking place, thereby conferring on it a reality it might not otherwise have. It then becomes possible to both criticise the paradigm of the clash at the level of theory, and to still implicitly endorse it at another level, in the evocation of an ever present threat. Bottici's analyses also show how the very idea of 'the West' can function as part of the same cluster of reciprocally reinforcing constructs – an 'imaginal' being caught up in cultural and political 'myths'.

What matters for my purposes here is the insight into the ways in which ideas, imagery and emotion can converge in rhetorical constructs to become, through repetition, prevailing assumptions, strengthened by circulation within social groups. They can produce or transform realities, rather than simply representing something that already exists independently of them. The 'clash of civilisations', the 'war on terror', the defence or repudiation of 'the West' – all can be seen as 'political myths' that feed off one another. They can, in some contexts, operate as harmless metaphors – as useful ways of referring briefly to complex phenomena. Yet, as constructs of collective imagining, they can also come to carry intense emotional associations – fuelled by fear, ignorance or malice, with real and tragic effects. In the case of this particular 'mythology', the power of the political rhetoric is underpinned by a common appropriation of the language of war.

The locution of a 'war on terror' acquired much of its initial effectiveness from a prior rhetorical configuration around the idea of a 'war on drugs'. Also in the mix is residue from older 'cold war' constructs. These layers of often repeated metaphors have a cumulative effect. Metaphors which might once have served to clarify thought and enliven communication can harden to become uncritical and elusive distortions in the understanding of complex situations.[6]

Not all clichés have politically significant effects. Yet it is illuminating to consider the processes by which rhetorical constructs can harden through repetition to the point where they appear to be literal statements of undeniable fact. Orin

Hargraves, in a helpful and entertaining analysis of such processes, has pointed out that it is not just the overuse of a term, or the verbosity of its users, that produces a cliché. Many idioms gain extremely high usage because they convey succinctly an idea that would demand more syllables to communicate literally. Thus, for example, the very common phrase 'shed light on' – used frequently, along with similar metaphorical expressions, in philosophical writing – remains efficient, effective and awkward to replace. Transitions from metaphor to cliché are more likely when a term is misapplied in the first place, and then frequently repeated in contexts where its application is dubious. In terms reminiscent of Derrida's talk of the 'contagiousness' of collective stupidity, Hargraves observes – in a wilfully vivid metaphor – that clichés have a *revenant* lifestyle; they flutter to life briefly on use, but with a virus-like ability to infect their recipients.[7]

When political mystification is added to these processes, there is collusion in accepting as unavoidable what may often be just one among many possible ways of seeing a problem or predicament. The treatments of *aporia* discussed earlier invoked a halt in active thinking, induced by a sense of having nowhere to move. As described by Spinoza, the experience of wonder involved the mind seeing no way forward, yet needing of its very nature to continue the activity of thinking. To put those thoughts together: where a mind comes to see that what blocks its path is not an impasse arising naturally in its own efforts to think, but a barrier erected by politically inspired mystification, then exposing this deadening delusion can itself constitute a political intervention.

So far, my discussion of the bearing of wonder and the experience of *aporia* on social critique has tracked a path from Spinoza's diagnosis of biblical narratives as fictions, and Burke's treatment of the power of words, through Sartre's and Derrida's engagement with Flaubert's lists of 'accepted ideas', to more recent strategies of demystification centred on ideas of 'social imaginaries' and 'political myths'. Let me now take a different trajectory – starting from Arendt's appropriation of Heidegger's 'wonder at the ordinary'. This was, as we have seen, a development that Arendt herself sketched – beginning from Socratic wonder, through reflection on Kant's third *Critique*, to the idea of wonder as connected with judgement as 'the most political' of the faculties of the human mind.

Arendt's Appropriation of Kant

Arendt herself was unabashed in appropriating past philosophical thought in the interest of engagement with her own political present. What she found impressive and inspiring in Kant's *Critique of Judgement* was not its obvious relations with aesthetic theory, but its less manifest relevance for thinking about judgement in relation to the political aspects of human life. This was, she thought, something the full significance of which lay beyond what Kant himself had in mind in writing the work. In her *Lectures on Kant's Political Philosophy*, she thus addresses herself to what she describes as 'a Kantian topic that, literally speaking, is non-existent – i.e., his non written political philosophy'. Her project was to 'try to suggest what Kant's political philosophy would have been like had he found the time and the strength to express if adequately'.[8]

Arendt's lectures, as we have seen, highlighted Kant's emphasis on human sociability as the key to understanding his treatment of the faculty of judgement. Sociability was for him the precondition for the operation of judgement, as the faculty which deals with the particular – as opposed to the grasp of general concepts. What is, in this sense, 'particular' can be a contingent fact of nature or an event in history; it is something specific, which elicits a collective response. Arendt suggests that this 'particularity' is something of eminent significance for the political aspects of human life.

Central to the political aspects of Kant's version of judgement was the idea of an 'enlargement of mind', accomplished by 'comparing our judgement with the possible rather than the actual judgement of others, and putting ourselves in the place of any other man' (p. 43).[9] Arendt's crucial insight here is that this expanded notion of sociability makes judgement dependent on another capacity – imagination. This 'enlargement' of thought involves imaginatively taking up a 'general standpoint' from which 'to look upon, to watch, to form judgements, or, as Kant himself says, to reflect upon human affairs' (p. 44).

On Arendt's reconstruction of a 'Kantian' political philosophy, the capacity for critical judgement, which is so crucial to political life, is to be understood through his analysis in the third *Critique* of 'reflective judgements of taste'. Those judgements involve sociability and a related capacity for detachment. That capacity arises from taking up a standpoint of 'disinterestedness', which nonetheless demands reference to the perspectives of others. We can now see more clearly how the form of 'detachment' that Arendt invokes here differs from what she saw as Heidegger's withdrawal from the political. Critical judgement, in her sense, demands an ability and willingness to adopt the impartial viewpoint of a spectator on human affairs: 'Judgment, and especially judgments of taste, always reflects upon others and their taste, takes their possible judgments into account. This is necessary because I am human and cannot live outside the company of men' (p. 67).

Such 'taking of others into account' was also central in the eighteenth-century concern with developing an objective basis for the critical evaluation of works of art or literature. There may seem a great difference between an 'aesthetic' and a 'political' stance on human affairs – between the pleasure engendered by contemplation of a beautiful object and, on the other hand, a state of political indignation or outrage. However, Arendt is talking, in both cases, of a shift to the position of spectator – a standpoint from which 'detachment' amounts not to indifference, but rather to a form of *engaged* thinking. That shared 'spectator' position makes for commonalities between impartial judgement on human affairs and, on the other hand, aesthetic appreciation – construed as a capacity for 'disinterested delight' in things. Yet the recognition of those commonalities is not meant to recast political judgement as mere aesthetic contemplation.

Arendt's reconstructions of a Kantian version of the kind of judgement involved in the political dimensions of human life are, as she herself acknowledges, sketchy. She is elaborating Kant's undeveloped insights into the kind of thinking that is done 'in company', drawing on them to piece together her own approach to judgement as 'the most political of human faculties'. Incomplete though this part of Arendt's treatment of 'the life of the mind' was, it does open up consideration of the connections between wonder as an aesthetic concept and its potential role in political consciousness.

Many of the recurring motifs we have seen in the philosophical history of wonder could be restated as markers in the uneven development of individual political awareness: the pause in thinking occasioned by exposure to the incongruous; the mixture of emotions in which the mind struggles to accommodate unexpected anomalies; the temporary stupor induced by the shock of recognition, which can readily turn into prolonged apathy; the effort to return to active thinking.

Arendt did not manage to pursue the implications of her envisaged treatment of judgement for the more directly political issues that concerned her. Yet there are some suggestive connections with some of those themes – with issues of individual and collective responsibility; with her controversial discussions of the deficiencies in engaged thinking manifested in the Eichmann trial; with the nascent notions of collective imagining which imbue her influential concept of 'natality'. In *The Human Condition*, she introduced the latter concept as a kind of second birth – a principle of beginning through which human beings become members of communities, born into burdens of responsibility for a past in which they did not yet exist, and hence drawn into the social narratives which shape individual thought.[10] The theme I want to pursue here is one where the political dimensions of the faculty of judgement are most evident, and of contemporary relevance – Arendt's engagement with issues associated with the mass movements of people in response to war, natural disasters and discrimination.

Thinking with Arendt about Refugees

In 1943, Arendt published, in the Jewish journal *Menohra*, a heartfelt essay on an experience she shared with many of her friends and acquaintances – that of being a refugee. In her times, she observed, the meaning of 'refugee' had changed. Refugees used to be persons driven to seek asylum because of their dissident acts or political opinions. The relatively narrow concept of 'rights to refuge', inherited from eighteenth-century declarations of the inalienable Rights of Man, no longer fitted the movements of large groups of people forced to flee – not because of acts or opinions directed against the policies of their own states, but solely because of their race or ethnic characteristics.

To be a refugee, Arendt drily remarked, now meant to be among those 'who have been so unfortunate as to arrive in a new country without means and have to be helped by Refugee Committees'. Contemporary history, she suggested, had produced a conceptual shift, though nobody wanted to know. She and her fellow exiles represented not only a new kind of refugee, but a new kind of human being: 'the kind that are put in concentration camps by their foes and in internment camps by their friends'.[11]

Arendt's essay focused on the anomalies and ironies of the situation of Jewish refugees in Second World War Europe. Central to their predicament was a dilemma of assimilation. The new arrivals were regarded in their host countries not only as 'prospective citizens', but also as 'enemy aliens'. Not surprisingly, the refugees themselves were ambivalent in responding to their situation: 'If we are saved, we feel humiliated, and if we are helped we feel degraded.'

Arendt's essay was both emotionally raw and ironic in tone. Yet it made some trenchant conceptual points, to which she returned in a more formal discussion of the situations of refugees in her first major book, *The Origins of Totalitarianism*, published in 1951. There she discussed the shifts of attention demanded between consideration of individual refugee cases for political asylum and, on the other hand, responses to the modern phenomenon of mass movements of whole groups of people. She pointed out that difficulties arose for the very idea of asylum once it became clear that the new twentieth-century forms of persecution were far too numerous to be handled by an unofficial practice designed for exceptional situations.

The issues raised by Arendt were not to do merely with the practicalities of processes designed to deal with exceptional cases having to adapt to larger numbers. There were also deeper conceptual issues at stake. To be a refugee was no longer to be an individual 'dissident', seeking protection from one state by seeking asylum in another. It was to be part of a mass movement of people in danger – not because of the opinions they expressed, but solely because of *what they were*.

Some of the conceptual aspects of Arendt's discussions of refugees have been taken up by the Italian philosopher, Giorgio Agamben. In an essay from 1993, discussing Arendt, he argued that the condition of modern refugees reflected significant shifts in the understanding of citizenship and of statehood. Agamben addressed what he saw as a paradox in the fact that, after the solemn invocations of human rights in the aftermath of the Second World War, the figure of the refugee, which should have embodied those rights *par excellence*, brought instead a conceptual crisis. Talk of 'inalienable rights' appealed to the supposed existence of 'a human being as such', bypassing considerations of statehood. The figure of the refugee became something more than a practically challenging presence at borders. It became a troubling 'border concept' – unattached to any specific identity. Refugees were an exception to the coupling of rights and statehood. Their presence evoked disturbing thoughts of a permanently resident mass of non-citizens.[12]

Today's mass movements of people are again challenging, not only the practicalities of protection and resettlement, but also the thought patterns we bring to understanding the issues. There are conceptual issues at stake here that go beyond the predicaments of systems under strain from the sheer force of numbers. Once again, we seem to be witnessing major shifts in the understanding of the very idea of a 'refugee'.

It lies beyond the scope of this book to seek to unravel the many argumentative anomalies that beset current debates on refugee issues. However, some aspects of the impasses that beset those debates do seem to relate directly to the understanding of wonder. The bewilderment that triggers wonder is not always an experience of delighted surprise. It can also take the form of shock or dismay at the realisation that our habitual expectations and responses no longer fit the political realities confronting us. The vehement clashes of indignation or outrage that have become a common feature of debates about refugee policy become more readily understandable in the light of unresolved conceptual tensions.

The images of millions of people on the move we are confronted with do not always fit ideas of refugee status developed after the Second World War. Those images do not fit neatly the defining categories of persecution agreed by the signatories to the UN Refugee Convention of 1951 – the year which also saw the publication of *The Origins of Totalitarianism*. The processes associated with that Convention – designed to meet the challenges of refugee movements of the time – are themselves now under strain. A system designed to evaluate individual claims for protection on the basis of specific criteria for group persecution – primarily race, religion, ethnicity – struggles to cope with the sheer volume of people on the move for what may be a complex mix of reasons, not all of which conform precisely to the Convention's requirements.

It is now the *asylum seeker*, rather than the *refugee*, that has become the focal point for conceptual confusion. The term itself signifies something unresolved or uncertain, in ways that go beyond the familiar realities of seeking asylum with no assurance of it being granted. The concept of asylum seeker now carries an inherent indeterminacy, which accrues from its implicit reference to the Convention criteria for establishing persecution. Asylum seekers are, by definition, not yet assessed as falling into what has become a narrower category – that of the refugee. Although their rights to due process in having their claims to refugee status considered are protected by the Convention, an aura of illegitimacy frequently surrounds them, especially if – as the Convention allows – they have crossed borders without prior authorisation. Their unresolved status on arrival is a potent source of division, even in signatory countries. Though potentially satisfying the recognised criteria for refugee status, they are often pre-emptively and pejoratively regarded as 'illegal' or as mere 'economic migrants'. A contrast between the supposedly good refugee and the bad asylum seeker has become a familiar motif in the political rhetoric of refugee policy, although it has no basis in refugee law.

Asylum seekers might or might not turn out to be 'genuine' refugees; but in this context 'genuine' has also become a loaded term. Asylum seekers who are absolutely genuine in their belief that they are fleeing mortal danger might yet not turn out to satisfy the relevant criteria of eligibility for protection. The status of 'refugee' cannot be determined by outside spectators. Nor can it really be self-evident to asylum seekers themselves. It depends on complex exercises of interpretation of a Convention. It may rest on nuanced judgements about the satisfaction of specific criteria, formulated in documents designed to respond to situations different from those that now govern the mass movements of people. There are also other sources of indeterminacy. 'Refugee' and 'economic migrant' are not necessarily exclusive categories. It is possible to be both impoverished and 'persecuted on grounds of race or religion'. Nor can impoverishment itself always be clearly separated out from a surrounding context of discrimination.

It is a striking feature of current debates on asylum seeker policy that the inherent uncertainties of the concept tend to be glossed over – or pre-emptively resolved – by all sides. Rather than being seen as a person seeking protection whose claim has yet to be evaluated, the asylum seeker is pre-judged as someone who has arrived, not just without prior authorisation, but with the purpose of making an *unjustified* claim. The implicit pre-emptive judgement encourages us to think that they have done something illicit in just coming – uninvited and unauthorised – to ask for consideration of their case for protection.

The inherent indeterminacy can also be occluded in the opposite direction – as when asylum seekers are described *en masse* as the world's 'most wretched' or 'most vulnerable'. Not all pre-emptive judgements are mistaken. It is not unreasonable to expect that, given the hazards and hardships of many of the journeys made, those who survive are likely to be found to have had compelling reasons to come. Yet the rival pre-emptive judgements yield a clash of competing spurious 'certainties', where there is as yet no certainty to be had. It is as if imagination has run off in different directions – throwing up competing schematic narratives, each moving all too quickly to a misleading clarity.

There are also other sources of conceptual slippage, which help to confuse current debate. Although there is in fact no illegality in an asylum seeker coming, unauthorised, to a Convention signatory country to ask to be considered for protection, many countries do have explicit legislation against 'people smuggling'. 'Unauthorised' boat arrivals, who may have resorted to (illegal) people smugglers as the only means of escape available, then enter a confused web of perception in which the illegal acts of the people smugglers seem to spread by contagion to the people they have transported. The unauthorised asylum seekers disappear into the category of illegal cargo. Worse, they can come to be seen as themselves aiming to do harm by breaching borders – despite their obviously having no intention of keeping their arrival concealed. Publicly seeking protection is, after all, often the whole point of an asylum seeker having made a dangerous journey.

It can seem that the sheer volume of current mass movements of people overwhelms the inherent indeterminacy of the concept of asylum seeker, and the nuanced conceptual distinctions through which human predicaments are supposed to be evaluated. Not surprisingly, it is a situation in which the operation of 'political myths' is rife. Understanding how those myths operate can help bring some much needed clarity to the issues. Mantras about 'border security' and 'those who seek to do us harm' are reinforced by older narratives of the 'war on terror'. The fact that many current asylum seekers are Muslim also fuels a hostile rhetoric of the 'Islamisation' of 'western' societies, which in turn draws on older ideas of a 'clash of civilisations'. Old narratives are simplistically extended to cover new events. Harsh, even physically violent, 'border control', exerted against asylum seekers fleeing war and terror, becomes an extension of the 'war on terror'. It is ironic that it has also come to symbolise a resolute defence of 'enlightened western values'.

Much of the rhetoric accompanying punitive reactions against harmless asylum seekers – in Australia, Europe, and more recently in the United States – can appear to exemplify what Derrida wryly described as the contagious effects of stupidity. Yet the vehement repudiation of these prevailing 'political myths' can itself get caught up in fruitless clashes of narratives and counter-narratives. Where disagreements take that form, it becomes inevitable that each side reconstructs the other's position as issuing from an apparent blindness to obvious facts – to the point where there is no room to move. One side makes accusations of a wilful denial of established human rights; the other alleges reckless disregard for national security, or a naive readiness to accept all comers across 'open borders'. It can seem that all it would take for a remedy is that the scales of stupidity should fall from our opponents' eyes to reveal the certainties that are manifest to us. Faced with this kind of impasse, it may be helpful to reflect on whether such clashes of apparent certainties might suggest that something is lacking in the thought patterns on both sides.

The vehement reiteration of competing certainties can close off possibilities of reframing the issues – of moving, as Arendt described it, into a space of detachment, where objective judgement is possible. What she called the 'sociability' of judgement involved comparing our own judgements with the possible – rather than the actual – judgements of others, by putting ourselves in the place of 'any other' judging mind. What she sketched was not a matter of polite recognition of the actual opinions of others. It need not involve a compromise of strongly held beliefs. But it does involve stepping back from apparent certainties in order to think in a different space – the space of judgement. The exposure of the competing narratives here is not a matter of alleging defective intelligence. What it does require is making space for a form of deliberative thinking which is not oriented to the reaching of exclusive certainties.

We have here come, by a different route, to the idea that intrigued Derrida in relation to Flaubert's lists of received opinions – that there is a kind of stupidity which is not a matter of flawed intellect or intelligence, but an inherent tendency of human thinking. Recognising that form of stupidity can open up a space in which real thinking can occur. Again, it is not just a matter of acknowledging what may be plausible in an actual rival point of view. It involves shifting to a shared space of detachment where other possible perspectives can be taken into account.

It was a major insight of Arendt's – undeveloped though it was – that the loss of the space of 'sociable' judgement is also the loss of a kind of wonder. It is the loss of a capacity to allow the movement between knowing and not-knowing which is crucial to the ongoing activity of the mind. Applied to the fraught impasses of the debate on asylum seeker policy, this admittedly sketchy notion of a shared space of judgement might hold a promise of something different from the current shouting across the abyss of competing certainties. It might open up possibilities of imagining constructive alternatives to those desperate journeys of the uninvited, which can seem so threatening to those to whom they come in the hope of finding help. The common mantras that insist that there are no alternatives to harsh policies of deterrence of 'illegal migration' often ignore – whether wilfully or not – practicable, more humane alternatives.

In the emotionally charged atmosphere of current polemic, it may seem that, challenged to produce better alternatives, the only appropriate response may be the one proffered in the Irish joke:

'I wouldn't start from here.' Humane alternatives that were once readily available may now appear blocked by the harsh deterrence measures already in place. Yet the reiteration of spurious certainties, fuelled by 'political myths', itself debilitates the free movement of imagination. In an open space of judgement, alternatives might cease to be unthinkable. Plato described the drawing of bad conceptual divisions as hacking at the beast of reality like a bad butcher, instead of carving it along the joints. Much of the current debate about asylum seeker policy rests on ill-formed, supposedly exhaustive divisions between 'strong border protection' and 'open borders'.

The conviction that there are indeed no alternatives to the manifest cruelty of harsh policies of deterrence may itself be one of the worst political delusions. A reimagining of possibilities – with a clear focus on the needs of refugees, as well as on the practicalities of their presence – might bring us to consider significant increases in official refugee resettlement places in Convention signatory countries. We might collectively consider breaking the nexus between places where the evaluation of asylum claims takes place, and the places where resettlement occurs. We might rethink regular migration programmes – including temporary worker visa arrangements – to give greater prominence to humanitarian considerations. We might consider new visa categories, which allow for safe travel to signatory countries for the purpose of making applications for protection. We might provide greater assistance to current 'host' countries for provision of health, education and work rights until refugees can either return home or move on – 'authorised' – for resettlement elsewhere.

More generally, we might rethink the assumption that deterrence of asylum seekers – rather than the provision of authorised safe pathways – is the best way of 'breaking the people smugglers' business model'. We might begin to reconsider the underlying assumptions that govern the evaluation of asylum claims, based on established criteria of persecution. We might then recognise that there is, increasingly, a variety of valid reasons that drive people to become refugees, as well as a multiplicity of ways of meeting their varied needs.

The emergence of a new category of 'failed asylum seeker' is one of the more disturbing manifestations of the shifting concept of 'refugee' in our times. Under the impact of massive increases in the numbers of people seeking protection, the application of Convention criteria of persecution is becoming ever more restrictive, while the 'processing' at borders becomes ever more cursory. Not all those who 'fail' the increasingly 'extreme' vetting processes can reasonably expect safety if 'refouled' to their country of origin.

The cliché-ridden political rhetoric that has become typical of responses to the mind-numbing images of refugee flows has become no less paralysing than the images themselves. Emotion, as well as imagination, seems to have fallen prey to the competing 'certainties'. There is, for example, the strange competition for moral superiority that has arisen around the place of compassion in asylum seeker policy. Compassion is appropriated on all sides. Some condemn, in its name, the harshness of policies centred on deterrence; others defend those same policies – also in the name of compassion.

In 'the drowning argument', which has gained credence in the defence of Australia's harsh policies of off-shore detention, the punitive treatment of those who survive dangerous sea voyages is presented as motivated by compassion towards indeterminate others who might otherwise attempt the journey. The destruction of the makeshift buildings of the Calais 'jungle' – populated by asylum seekers desperate to get to Britain – has likewise been described by local authorities as 'a humanitarian gesture'. Tacitus famously quoted a Caledonian rebel's description of the Romans as using the lying name of 'government' when they create a desolation and call it peace. It seems we now create desolate detention centres to discourage desperate asylum seekers – and call it compassion.

Rather than rejecting appeals to compassion, supporters of policies of deterrence often claim that these policies are compassionate despite their harshness – or, indeed, that they are compassionate precisely in being harsh. With all sides claiming the moral high ground, we may well wonder whether appeals to compassion are playing any constructive role in the debate. On some ways of thinking, that confusion is really just what we might expect from admitting anything so emotional or subjective in the first place.

Sometimes the shock of confrontation with particular images can jar so much with established narratives that it prompts at least a brief rethink – as happened in 2015 with the horrifying image of a dead Syrian child on a Turkish beach, amidst the influx of boats of asylum seekers trying to reach Europe. Suddenly, it was as if attitudes had changed overnight: offers of resettlement were made; promises given of a warm welcome. Yet the received narrative quickly reasserted its dominance. The image was absorbed into the rhetoric of 'tough compassion' as a rallying call against any softening of strong border-control measures. Something similar happened in response to the earlier horrific images of shipwrecked asylum seekers off Australia's Christmas Island. An outpouring of goodwill towards asylum seekers was quickly reabsorbed into an appropriation of the images to strengthen the rhetoric of deterrence, rather than prompting renewed efforts to provide others with safe alternative paths to a future.

Does compassion really have a place in policy deliberations that demand objectivity? Should it be admitted at all into the arena of clear-headed policy making? In the second chapter of her book *On Revolution*, where she addresses 'the social question', Arendt questions the credentials of compassion as a 'political virtue'.[13] She argues that compassion is not unlike love in that it tends to abolish the distance – the 'in between' – of human intercourse. It is a point in keeping with her stress on the idea of 'the public space' as the core of political consciousness; and also with her resistance to the role that Rousseau gave to compassion as establishing and confirming the 'natural bond' between human beings as the basis of society. For Arendt, although the appeal to compassion evokes a desire to share in the suffering of others, treating it as a political virtue in fact depersonalises 'the people'.

Unreliable though compassion may be as a benchmark of policy – or as an indicator of public virtue – it is nonetheless hard to imagine that emotion could reasonably be left out of the consideration of the wretchedness accompanying current mass movements of people without distorting that reality. To claim to be doing so in the name of detachment or objectivity is to distort the philosophical history of those ideals. An important thread in that history is the recognition that intellect, imagination and emotion are interrelated, and that they interact in ways that resist any sharp separations between them. Spinoza saw this – in treating wonder as something inherent in the activity of thinking. Kant saw it – in insisting on the harmonising of the faculties of mind, which generate emotional intensity in their interaction. Eighteenth-century theorists of aesthetic judgement also glimpsed the possibility of a form of objectivity which depended, not on transcending emotion and imagination, but on understanding their operations and interactions.

Arendt tried to appropriate the structure of Kantian aesthetic judgement and apply it more generally to the political aspects of judgement. Her insight has made it possible to see that politically relevant forms of objectivity might not only accommodate emotion but also require it. It is not incidental that the cast of mind she sketched as belonging with Socratic wonder was described as 'passionate' or 'engaged' thinking. Objectivity of this kind does not involve setting emotion aside; on the contrary, it demands a reflective synthesis of intellect, emotion and imagination in what she called that most 'political' of faculties – judgement. Our currently impoverished political thinking might be enriched by trying to regain some of those lost connections.

Notes

1 George Orwell, *A Collection of Essays* (Orlando: Harcourt Books, 1981), pp. 166–7.
2 See, for example, his essay, 'Radical Imagination and the Social Instituting Imaginary', in Gillian Robinson and John Rundell, eds, *Rethinking Imagination* (London and New York: Routledge, 1994), pp. 136–54.
3 Charles Taylor, *Modern Social Imaginaries* (Durham, NC: Duke University Press, 2004), p. 25.
4 Chiara Bottici, *Imaginal Politics: Images Beyond Imagination and the Imaginary* (New York: Columbia University Press, 2014).
5 Sartre, *The Family Idiot*, p. 602.
6 For interesting discussion of the rhetorical origins of the 'war on drugs', see Johann Hari, *Chasing the Scream: The First and Last Days of the War on Drugs* (New York: Bloomsbury, 2015); and, on the rhetoric of the 'war on terror', Arun Kundnani, *The Muslims are Coming: Islamaphobia, Extremism,*

and the Domestic War on Terror (London and New York: Verso, 2014), especially Chapter 3, pp. 89–115.
7 Orin Hargraves, *It's Been Said Before: A Guide to the Use and Abuse of Clichés* (Oxford: Oxford University Press, 2014), p. 10.
8 Arendt, *Lectures on Kant's Political Philosophy*, p. 19. Further page references will be given in the main text.
9 The reference is to Kant, *Critique of Judgement*, Sec. 40.
10 For an interesting extended discussion of the political ramifications of Arendt's treatment of judgement, see Ronald Beiner's Interpretive Essay, 'Hannah Arendt on Judging', in Arendt, *Lectures on Kant's Political Philosophy*, pp. 89–156.
11 Hannah Arendt, 'We Refugees', republished in Marc Robinson, ed., *Altogether Elsewhere: Writers in Exile* (Boston: Faber & Faber, 1994), pp. 110–19.
12 Giorgio Agamben, 'Beyond Human Rights', in Paolo Virno and Michael Hardt, eds, *Radical Thought in Italy: A Potential Politics* (Minneapolis: University of Minnesota Press, 1996); also included in Agamben's *Means Without End: Notes on Politics* (Minneapolis and London: University of Minnesota Press, 2000).
13 Hannah Arendt, *On Revolution* [1963] (London: Penguin Books, 2006), pp. 49–105.

9

Wonder and Transcendence

The sense of awe historically associated with wonder has given it close connections with religion. Not all religions have strong associations with the idea of transcendence. But what happens to wonder when old beliefs in a supernatural realm cease to be part of a culture's 'ordinary' understanding of the world, and of the place of human beings within it? The claim is sometimes made, by contemporary defenders of the importance of religion in western societies, that life in a 'secularised' world is a life without wonder. The demise of a capacity for wonder, along with other alleged losses – of a sense of purpose, of meaning – is sometimes invoked as a sign of the depletion of human consciousness under conditions of modern secularity. What exactly is it that is supposedly lost when wonder loses its habitual connections with religious belief directed towards the supernatural?

Wonder and the Secular

For a start, there is a terminological ambiguity that needs to be kept in mind – the differences between 'secularism' and 'the idea of the secular' in relation to belief in some transcendent order.

Charles Taylor has made the point persuasively with reference to moral consciousness under conditions of western secular modernity. In his book, *A Secular Age*, he argued that the modern idea of the secular should not be construed as the mere absence of belief in the supernatural. What is at stake is the issue of what role is played by that belief in the collective life of a society. On his account, the modern idea of the secular involves a rethinking of the conceptual underpinnings of morality, shedding the supernatural order as superfluous for those purposes.[1]

In this context, Taylor argued, the idea of the secular is not a mere residue of the loss or 'subtraction' of transcendence. Rather, it involves a 'radical immanentising' of the basis of moral consciousness – a conceptual shift that amounts to 'one of the great realisations in the history of human development'.[2] The rejection of the 'subtraction' model is a central theme throughout Taylor's extended analysis of what he calls our 'secular age'. Part of his point is that the modern idea of the secular opens up the possibility of a shared conceptual space between religious belief and unbelief. The 'immanentising' of the foundations of morality displaces the supernatural from that role, but it does not thereby challenge religious belief.

The idea of the secular, thus understood, can be embraced equally by those who believe in a transcendent realm – a supernatural order – and by those who do not. It is different from a common use of 'secularism', which carries connotations of repudiation of religious belief. One of the strengths of the modern idea of the secular is that it acknowledges a shared public domain of communication and contestation, in which religiously based moral codes can be acknowledged – provided they do not harm others – while no longer being accepted as universally binding. At the core of that ideal is the acceptance of intra-human – rather than divinely authorised – bases of moral judgement. In that respect, the idea of 'secular' moral consciousness is akin to older political ideas of the secular, which drew boundaries between duties to Church and to State. The idea of the secular thus provides a template for the understanding of differences over moral issues under modern conditions of cultural diversity.

In its origins, *the secular* is a religious construct. In Christian thought it developed in the context of a temporal distinction. Secular time – the *saeculum* – was the time preceding the redemptive transformation anticipated in Christ's 'second coming', which would subsume the 'temporal' into the 'eternal' life to come. It is an ironic twist in intellectual history that an idea whose content was provided by religious belief should have come, in our own times, to be seen as indicative of a morally dangerous rejection of belief in the supernatural. Taylor's distinction between the religiously neutral 'idea of the secular' and the anti-religious idea of 'secularism' can help clarify the terms of debates about the place of religion in 'secular' societies.

Ideas of the secular are not the preserve of any particular religion, but developments within societies influenced by Christianity played an important part in the formation of the concept in western thought. At its core is the notion of a shared public space of rational argumentation, deliberation and reflective judgement. In culturally diverse societies, that space is rightly seen as a bulwark against the encroachment of religious fundamentalism, in all its varieties.

To claim that wonder depends on a belief in transcendence is, on the face of it, even more implausible than to suggest that divine commands are the sole possible basis for morality. Wonder at the natural world surely remains possible when belief in anything transcending it is rejected. Yet there are issues that arise about the interconnections of wonder and religious awe that may well appear to lend some credibility to the idea that the demise of religious belief has brought with it, at any rate, a dilution or impoverishment in the experience of wonder. Might there be, here too, conceptual shifts in the understanding of wonder, which go beyond a simple model of 'subtraction' of belief in the supernatural? If there is a general waning of belief in a supernatural order — the reality of which suffuses the 'natural' world — does that change the quality of the experience of wonder?

The parallels with moral consciousness may help us better articulate the issues here; and there has indeed been some overlap between consideration of wonder and of morality in the history of philosophy. Some eighteenth-century discussions of the distinction between the sublime and the beautiful addressed the relevance of either or both of these 'feelings' to the formation of moral consciousness. There are, however, some major differences between moral consciousness and a sense of wonder, which make talk of a conceptual shift to a 'secular' version of wonder more confusing than enlightening. In the case of moral consciousness, the issue of transcendence is about the *basis* of moral judgement: does it derive from supernatural sources or from 'natural' — intra-human — ones? Issues of the grounding of moral authority — and of justifying the objectivity of moral judgements — remain of contemporary interest. In trying to understand wonder the issue is, rather, of how to *describe* that experience and its role in human life. It is not a matter of how to *justify* it.

Eighteenth-century thinkers were concerned with finding an objective base for aesthetic judgements — with establishing the objectivity of 'standards of taste', variable though the judgements of particular critics of art might be. There seems no comparable contemporary felt need to find something akin to universally acceptable grounds for distinctively 'aesthetic' judgements. There are, nonetheless, some ways in which keeping in mind Taylor's distinction with regard to the secular can help us get to grips with what is at stake in asking whether changing attitudes to transcendence can affect either the experience or the understanding of wonder.

'Absolute Ego' and Transcendence

I talked earlier of an 'eclipse' of wonder under the intensity of the idea of the sublime – as if wonder-at-the-ordinary needed to come out from under that mesmerising glare, if it is to regain something of its old status in the life of the mind. That story of the power of the sublime is, in some ways, the same story as that of wonder's changing relations with ideas of transcendence, and hence with religion. For clarification of those changes – and of what they might mean for wonder in the present and the future – we must now return briefly to what became of wonder under the influence of German Idealism and Romanticism. The core issue here is the role played by the German Idealists' treatment of the idea of 'the Absolute' and its associations with infinity.[3]

Kant's treatment of the mind's efforts to grasp the infinite centred on a distinction fundamental to all three of his *Critiques*: his famous differentiation of the realm of unknowable 'Noumena', or 'things in themselves', from that of 'Phenomena' – what is known under the determining conditions of human understanding. In this context, Kant emphasises the impossibility of *transcendent* objects of human understanding. Central to his version of a 'critical' philosophy was his insistence that its goal was not to access knowledge of things as they are in themselves; it was, rather to understand the *transcendental* conditions of human knowledge and experience – that is, the conditions under which objects of human knowledge are possible.

Kant did not regard this shift from the *transcendent* to the *transcendental* as inconsistent with acknowledging and describing the mind's persistent efforts to reach beyond its inevitable limits. In the *Critique of Practical Reason*, he talks of an endless striving for perfection; and we have seen that his account of the sublime in the *Critique of Judgement* invoked an effort of the imagination to reach beyond the necessity of its own limitations. Yet that yearning for complete knowledge, and the associated struggle to stretch imagination beyond its natural limits, were both shaped by – and indeed intelligible only through – the limitations he imposed on that exercise. For Kant, there is no access to complete knowledge, no matter how hard we try; nor are there any transcendent sublime objects awaiting a successful completion of our efforts to know.

Kant's emphasis, in relation to knowledge, was thus on what *can* be known, and on clarifying the conditions under which that knowledge is possible. In the thought of Romantic Idealism, the emphasis shifts. The striving towards – and yearning for – the infinite becomes the main game. The proper goal of the mind's struggles is now the Absolute, construed as *Absolute Ego*, in which the human mind finds its own destiny. For Fichte it becomes a metaphysical principle of existence. As Hegel describes it in his *Lectures on the History of Philosophy*, '[Fichte] maintained the ego to be the absolute principle, so that from it, the direct and immediate certainty of self, all the matter in the universe must be represented as produced.'[4] In its popular version, as rendered by Hegel, this becomes: 'All existence is living and active in itself, and there is no other life than Being, and no other Being than God; God is thus absolute Being and Life.'[5]

Arthur O. Lovejoy, in one of his several essays on the history of Romanticism, lyrically described that shift in emphasis, facilitated by Fichte's 'metaphysical principle', by saying that the very nature of all existence came to be construed as 'an infinite and insatiable striving of the Absolute Ego, whereby it first sets up the external world as an obstacle to its own activity, and then gradually but endlessly triumphs over this obstacle'.[6] The connotations of 'striving' resonate with several motifs we have seen in the philosophical history of wonder. In Plato's *Republic*, metaphors of struggle for an ever more adequate understanding of supersensible 'Forms' complement the *Theaetetus* account of wonder as mental agitation, directed towards knowledge.[7] Romantic notions of endless yearning after the infinite are redolent with those Platonic themes, as well as with Aristotelian notions of the mind's longing for knowledge as its natural 'end' or purpose.

We have also already seen some important connections between Romanticism and the philosophy of Spinoza, some of which were recognised at the time – whether to be celebrated or deplored. Crucially, there was controversy over whether – and which – Romantic theorists should be seen as influenced by Spinoza's alleged 'pantheism'.

Clearly, there are Spinozist overtones in Fichte's principle that both the world and the mind which struggles to know it are aspects of the one 'Absolute Ego'. We saw in an earlier chapter that Spinoza's theory of the world as the total expression of God under the attribute of matter – corresponding completely to its expression under the attribute of thought – resonated strongly with Romantic thinkers, even if they misconstrued what it was supposed to mean.

Spinoza's philosophy answered to a desire to resolve what Romantic Idealism saw as a dilemma in the understanding of selfhood: how to avoid either having the knowing self disappear into the known world, or, on the other hand, having the world disappear into an idealist version of the self. The theorists of Romanticism offered an imaginative rethinking of some aspects of Spinoza's philosophy, and that intellectual context allowed a flourishing of ideas of the sublime which Spinoza himself would not have endorsed.

The issue I want now to address more directly is this: what happens to wonder in the Romantic development of the idea of the infinite into that of Absolute Ego? If the upshot of Romantic Idealist thought is indeed – as Hegel represented it – that there is no other being than God, there is then no longer a realm of transcendence which could be coherently construed as acting causally on either mind or matter. If there remains only the distinction between less and more developed stages of organisation, ideas of a transcendent or supernatural realm seem to disintegrate.

Wonder at the extraordinary degree of organisation of matter remains possible within this conceptual configuration. What passes within it as an individual mind may well wonder at the complexity of higher stages of development than itself; and, from a limited perspective within it, it may well be possible to wonder at the idea of the whole. What seems no longer possible, though, is to conceive of Nature as suffused with intimations of a transcendent realm beyond it.

That loss of a world suffused with transcendence may well seem a significant change for the understanding of wonder. It gives rise to a question as to how to conceptually locate wonder in a world that is no longer seen as transcended by a different ream of the supernatural. Was the idea of the sublime itself a secularised version of wonder – wonder without transcendence? Or is it, rather, that the idea of the sublime came to substitute in secular consciousness for the religious awe that had previously been directed to the supernatural?

We are in deep waters here. They are about to get deeper before delivering us back to solid ground. We need to now look more closely at the beginnings of the Romantic sublime in the intricate passages of the 'Analytic of the Sublime' in Kant's *Critique of Judgement*. Kant was addressing questions about the basis of objectivity of aesthetic judgements; but in doing so he also offered an account of the role of the Noumenal – the inaccessible 'things in themselves' – in relation to human experience and knowledge. That account bears more generally on our question of the relations between the experience of the sublime and the notion of transcendence. Fortunately, some of the hard work in disentangling what is important for our purposes has been done in a close reading of the relevant passages by Jean-François Lyotard, in his *Lessons on the Analytic of the Sublime*, first published in 1991.[8]

Lyotard on the Violence of the Sublime

Lyotard suggested that for us now, looking back on Romanticism, these sections of the third *Critique* have a significance beyond what Kant himself could have foreseen. Kant's version of the sublime, on this reading, stands out as not properly part of the unified project of the three *Critiques*, which we have already seen articulated in Deleuze's *Kant's Critical Philosophy:* the account of the interrelations, interactions and eventual harmonising of the mind's faculties. For Lyotard, the sublime stands out as a specific concern of 'aesthetic' judgement; and Kant's task is to offer a 'transcendental critique' of the kind of 'communicability' which he saw as demanded by that specific form of judgement.

Lyotard's vivid summation of this special position of the Kantian sublime is that it represents 'a sudden blazing' outside Kant's wider story of human reason's coming to maturity in the higher reaches of ethical consciousness. Kant's contrasted category – 'the beautiful' – did have a part to play in that story of the 'departure from childhood', which he saw instantiated in the gradual processes of enlightenment under way in his own time. That story of progress and hope for the future was filled out in Kant's political essays, which were discussed in Arendt's *Lectures on Kant's Political Philosophy*. On Lyotard's reading of the 'Analytic of the Sublime', the Kantian sublime is not part of that story: 'Thus it is that it acquired a future and addresses us still, we who hardly hope in the Kantian sense' (p. 55).

Arendt's reading of the *Critique of Judgement* highlighted the communal, 'sociable' aspects of Kantian judgement, thus drawing from it a political relevance that Kant had not himself spelled out. Lyotard's reading – focused more directly on the 'Analytic of the Sublime' passages – emphasises, in contrast, what is specific to aesthetic judgement. It addresses, in particular, Kant's treatment of what is required for aesthetic feelings to be objectively communicable.

Lyotard observes that – whatever Kant himself might say to the contrary – his description of the feelings of delight at stake in the sublime closely follows Burke's (p. 24). Where the difference lies is in Kant's concern with a 'transcendental' critique of distinctively aesthetic judgement. For Lyotard, that makes

Kant's treatment of the sublime here different, not only from the merely 'empirical' approach that Kant attributes to Burke, but also from accounts which address the issue of 'communicability' only as a common feature of 'sociability'.

It may seem an esoteric point of interpretation of the role of the sublime in Kant's complex argumentative structure. Yet it has significant implications for understanding the notion of the sublime in relation to earlier versions of wonder. For it gives an explicit place to the idea of transcendence in explaining the communicability of aesthetic judgements. On Lyotard's account, the Kantian sublime is oriented towards transcendence – despite the fact that, in his critical philosophy as a whole, the human mind has no access to any transcendent object of knowledge.

What then is this specific character of aesthetic judgement that gives it an orientation towards an unreachable transcendence? Deleuze talked of struggle and conflict in his treatment of the relations between the Kantian faculties of Imagination, Understanding and Reason. In Lyotard's reading, that struggle takes on a more violent intensity, centred on the mind's unquenchable desire for limitlessness – for infinity. The Kantian feeling of the sublime involves, he suggests, 'a double defiance'. On the one hand, Imagination, at the limits of *what* it can present, 'does violence to itself in order to present *that* it can no longer present'. On the other hand, Reason, for its part, seeks unreasonably to violate its own prohibition on finding objects corresponding to its concepts in sensible intuition. 'In these two aspects, thinking defies its own finitude, as if fascinated by its own excessiveness. It is this desire for limitlessness that it feels in the sublime "state": happiness and unhappiness' (p. 55).

There are intimations of self-violation in the unfolding of this drama of the violence implicit in the feeling of the sublime.

Lyotard articulates it through reflection on the crucial contrast, which we have already seen in an earlier chapter, between Kant's beautiful and sublime: the one is concerned with form; the other, with utter formlessness. For Lyotard that becomes the key to grasping a special affinity between the sublime and Reason.

On Kant's analysis, there is – for both Understanding and Reason – an 'indeterminacy' in the effort to think the sublime. However, Lyotard points out that for Reason there is another level of indeterminacy, which sets it apart from the Understanding. Here, it is not just that there is an inevitable inadequacy in the presentation of an unlimited object. What is at stake in Reason's effort is that it *must not* be able to succeed. Rather, it must only make the attempt: 'In the case of the sublime, the without-form immediately suggests a concept of speculative reason, for the object of such a concept is by definition forbidden presentation and there is no presentation without form' (pp. 58–9).

The upshot of Lyotard's complex but clear-headed analysis of the interplay between Kantian Imagination, Understanding and Reason is that Reason's dominance in relation to the sublime is not a superiority in capacity to reach objects of knowledge denied to the other faculties. For Kant, Reason reaches no objects of knowledge; its concern is not with knowledge. It's affinity with the sublime resides, rather, in its capacity to indicate a 'presence' which is not knowledge. What then is it? The feeling of the sublime does not lead on to knowledge. Yet its exclusion from knowledge, rather than being a sign of weakness, is a source of strength: 'The powerlessness of the imagination becomes the *sign* of the omnipotence of reason' (p. 94). In excluding itself from knowledge, Reason asserts the power of its ideas as capable of pointing to the unknowable realm of the Noumenal.

This apparently perverse affirmation by Reason of its own power – in the face of its self-imposed exclusion from knowledge – is intensely emotional. What Lyotard describes here is not a calm interpretation of the meaning of signs. The doomed struggle to think the sublime involves a 'violent and ambivalent' emotion on 'the occasion of the formless' (p. 97). On this reading of Kant, there are intimations here of what will later become the Romantic mood of endless longing for the unattainable. The soul-stirring exaltation inspired by the sublime involves a recognition by thought that it is 'destined for the absolute' (p. 120). Yet, rather than being an unreachable external goal, this destination is to be found in thought itself – in the recognition that 'there is thought'. 'This is what "the voice of Reason" says in sublime feeling, and this is what is truly exalting' (p. 122).

Reason thus claims dominance in an arduous inner struggle; but this is not a conflict that admits of any real resolution. Nor can there be any allaying of what is fearful in it. The feeling of the sublime arises in a violent interaction between the faculties of the mind – each intent on stretching beyond its limit. There is no external goal to be achieved, and hence no resolution of the conflict. The dissonance is inherent in the feeling of the sublime itself. 'The most difficult and subtle trait to decipher in sublime feeling is the extreme dissonance between the powers of thought, which is felt as the sublime feeling's supreme consonance with itself' (p. 147).

Lyotard labels the affective charge of the Kantian feeling of the sublime as an affectual *differend* – an intense opposition, a resistance which brings both terror and exaltation (p. 149). Thought is here aware of a presence, but one which is not accompanied by 'presentation'. The sublime, thus construed, is a *sign* of the absolute – an intimation, rather than an apprehension of it. 'The absolute is never there, never given in a presentation, but it is always "present" as a call to think beyond the "there". Ungraspable, but unforgettable. Never restored, never abandoned' (p. 150).

The language of this rendering of Kant's 'Analytic of the Sublime' – with its evocations of awe, terror and exaltation – may sound like that of religious experience. Yet there is in it no expression of hope for divine deliverance from danger – or even of divine solicitude for human well-being. The feeling of the sublime is thought's recognition of its own powers and its own limits; and, above all, of the intense struggle between its different faculties in their efforts to reach beyond their limits. As Lyotard sums it up: there is thinking – and this is how thinking must be. The feeling of the sublime is thought's exalted recognition of its own reality.

Lyotard's reading makes it clear that Kant, in analysing the feeling of the sublime, was not theorising religious awe as it might be experienced by religious believers. Kant had talked in his 'Analytic of the Sublime' of a Savoyard peasant – 'simple-minded and, for the most part, intelligent' – who had unhesitatingly 'called all lovers of snow-mountains fools'.[9] He was not giving sophisticated religious believers advice about how they should feel about the supernatural, any more than he was advising the peasant how to feel about the beauty of his mountains. What he was talking of, rather, was how a mind might feel which has attained insight into what it is for there to be human thinking.

Kant himself insisted that he was not trying to provide an 'empirical' account of everyday experiences of wonder, however intense they might be. Lyotard fills out that disclaimer, presenting Kant as offering an account – for those capable of understanding it – of the interplay between faculties in a unified human mind, shaping up to a Noumenal realm that it can never claim to know. The reading retains, on Kant's behalf, a lurking presence of something transcendent in the feeling of the sublime – even if only as 'unpresented'. It involves the mind reaching towards something of another order, orienting itself to it – at the very least, thinking 'as if' it is in its presence.

What can all this show us about the relations between wonder and religious belief, under conditions of modernity? Lyotard's reading plays up those aspects of the Kantian sublime that facilitated the transition to Romanticism. It also illuminates ways in which some notion of transcendence might be accommodated to lack of religious belief. Kant's analysis of the sublime demands no prior assumptions about the existence of a supernatural order. It could be played out under the aegis of a shared fiction of a Noumenal realm – an exercise in 'As If' – which demands no assured belief in any transcendent objects actually existing beyond human thought. Indeed, an acknowledged lack of knowledge of such things is what the sublime is all about.

Yet, in the lack of any such shared commitment to a supernatural order, do we have any use for the sublime? If we remove all reference to transcendence – to the Noumenal, to the Absolute – can we make sense of the struggles of the mind in shaping up to that 'unpresented presence'? If transcendence is just a shared fiction, what becomes of the struggle, the terror, the exaltation? What really remains of the sublime? Does it become nothing more than a hollow intensity of feeling – a groundless excitement?

After the Sublime

Kant himself warned in the *Critique of Judgement* against a condition he distinguished from the feeling of the sublime – an 'enthusiasm', which he described as akin to delirium, a state which 'cannot merit any delight on the part of reason'.[10] He cautioned, more generally, against confusing the feeling of the sublime with any one particular emotional content. Lyotard, commenting on these passages, emphasises the importance of the warning: 'Any emotion, any subjective "state" of thought can pass over into the sublime: anger, desperation, sadness, admiration, and even "freedom from affection", or apathy, a state of disaffection, can become sublime' (p. 154).

Again, for Lyotard the crucial point is that the sublime arises from an intense interplay of faculties; the mere intensity of feeling is not enough. What gives the sublime its 'nobility' is its connections with a way of thinking that demands an extremity of inner struggle in the effort to present what must ever resist presentation. Hence, as Kant says, 'faint-hearted' or exhausted despair is not sublime; only the rage of forlorn hope.

It may well seem strange to talk – except in irony – of a sublime apathy while resisting the possibility of a sublime enthusiasm. However, for Kant apathy has the advantage of having 'the delight of pure Reason on its side'. Having Reason in the mix is supposed to save the intensity of the sublime from the hazards of mere 'enthusiasm', allowing its profound nobility to be distinguished from groundless fervour.

It is interesting to note here that for Kant the appeal to Reason also puts some restraint on talk of the 'sublime nobility' of the soldier. Yet he did nonetheless see something sublime in war itself – provided it is conducted 'with order and a sacred respect for the rights of civilians'. Carried on in such a manner, he said, war gives nations that engage in it 'a stamp of mind only the more sublime the more dangers to which they are exposed, and which they are able to meet with fortitude'.[11]

Such painstaking concern with the rightful allocation of the honorifics of the sublime – either by Kant himself or by Lyotard on his behalf – may well strike contemporary readers as quaint. As Agacinski said, 'we are not sublime!' In the eighteenth century, David Hume had already struck a cautionary note, in his *Inquiry Concerning the Principles of Morals*, about the desire to emulate in more modern times ancient ideals of 'greatness of mind', which he described, citing Longinus, as 'echoing in or imagined by, the idea of the sublime'. Hume acknowledged that there is great charm in the reverberations of the sublime in ancient poetic representations of magnanimity, courage or disdain of fortune: 'Among the ancients, the heroes in philosophy as well as those in war and patriotism have a grandeur and force of sentiment which astonishes our narrow souls, and is rashly rejected as extravagant and supernatural.' Yet, he insisted with a touch of irony at the expense of that tolerance of extravagance, there is also much to recommend the rival modern ideals of social virtues such as humanity, clemency, order and tranquillity.[12]

Not being sublime, we may be more likely to identify with Hume's modern ideals of the social virtues than with ancient 'greatness of mind'. Yet the resonances of the sublime are still with us. It was probably inevitable that Kant's complex unifying model of the human mind would splinter, so that the different elements in that grand synthesis of 'discordant accord' would go their separate ways. The restraints exerted by Kantian Reason receded. What remained was a confused, overexcited sense of awe, dread and exaltation — experienced as a haunting sense of loss of something intense and noble.

The great charm of the sublime lingers in contemporary consciousness — mingled with older reverberations of religious awe from times long before philosophical thinkers had begun to reflect on wonder. The allure of the sublime continues, even if we no longer know what sense to make of it. Not surprisingly, it continues to exert a strong pull on the imagination. Stretching the imagination to its limits was, after all, what the sublime was supposed to do. Yet it is perhaps unfortunate that the intensity and excitement associated with the sublime has proved so long-lasting a component in what has become the common understanding of wonder.

Kant's cautious endorsement of the sublimity of war lingers in the contemporary honouring of its noble sacrifices, along with his acknowledgement of the desirability of avoiding civilian casualties — now redescribed, with Orwellian echoes, as 'collateral damage'. The exultation of the feeling of the sublime echoes especially in the rhetoric of contemporary religious fundamentalism. Its apparent rigidities of religious observance can seem at odds with the wild formlessness we have seen in ideas of the sublime. Kant himself warned that if enthusiasm is comparable to delirium, fanaticism may be compared to mania. 'Of these', he said, 'the latter is least of all compatible with the sublime, for it is *profoundly* ridiculous.'[13] The exhilaration, bordering on violence, that Lyotard found in the Kantian sublime, does nonetheless still reverberate in religiously inspired extremism. The notion of a sublime nobility — enacted in its highest form in 'martyrdom' — is an element in terrorist recruitment strategies.

Among the many things involved in what has come to be known, within culturally diverse societies, as 'radicalisation' may well be a sense of the loss of something once directly associated with ideas of the sublime: intimations of transcendence; the aspiration to 'noble' self-sacrifice; a merging of individuality into some higher cause, some higher form of selfhood. Perhaps the vulnerability of the young to 'radicalisation' is – at least some of the time – due to a hankering after the sublime, in the lack of viable and sustainable forms of wonder.

The wonder that has shed its associations with transcendence cannot deliver a sense of the world suffused with a higher reality. It cannot convey the idea of a continuity between natural and supernatural. Augustine talked in his *City of God* of being entranced by the wondrous quality of plenteous light in its effects on the bright colours of birds and the great spectacle of the many-coloured sea. He could see in the effects of light on colours an instance – as well as a symbol – of the suffusion through the natural world of the divine power of its Creator. Wonder without transcendence does not express that vision. Yet nor is the wonder experienced in a 'secular' response to Nature experienced as a truncated version of something fuller or richer. It is a 'deprivation' only in the eyes of those who do express their wonder in terms of a belief in transcendence. Such expressions of wonder are appropriate – for those who do believe in the supernatural. Yet the response can be understood without sharing the belief.

Augustine's eloquent expression of his wonder at the 'natural' world is not lost on imaginative readers who do not happen to believe in his God. 'Objective communicability' does not presuppose shared actual belief. We can struggle to see the world objectively – and wonder at what we see – without yearning for an all-encompassing perspective on it, or clinging to the false reassurance of the fictions that masquerade as certainties.

A more nuanced understanding of the relations between wonder, imagination and religious belief might also help clarify some of the issues, around which current debate is polarised, concerning the place of Islam in culturally diverse 'secular' societies. The power of ideas of the secular to facilitate connections across difference, in a shared 'public' space of informed rational debate, operates across religious beliefs as well as between the religious and the non-religious.

Polemics around the supposed conflict between Islam and ideals associated with 'western' ideas of the secular frequently presume a rigidity of adherence to dogma — and to a literal interpretation of sacred texts — on the part of Muslims, which sets them apart from other citizens. They are then expected to prove their 'moderation'. The Syrian philosopher, Sadik Al-Azm, has observed that such attitudes ignore the long history of Islam's accommodation to differing environments and shifting political circumstances. He argues persuasively, in several essays on the issue, that there is nothing in principle to prevent historical Islam from coming to terms with, and making itself compatible with, secular humanism, democracy and modernity.[14]

Rethinking wonder can play a part in responding to the conceptual challenges of life in culturally diverse 'secular' societies. For wonder concerns attitudes towards difference and sameness. How we think of it is bound up with our attitudes towards the recognition of cultural differences amidst the commonalities of shared humanity. It can affect how we respond to vexed issues arising from the shifting understanding of 'multiculturalism' — issues of assimilation, integration, segregation and inclusion.

At times of rapid social change, the many postures of wonder are enacted in the eruption of the unexpected — the shock of the new. The bewilderment, the giddying excitement, the statue-like gaping, the awe and the terror at the unknown, the retreat to the familiar — they are all there, played out in the everyday dramas of lives exposed to the exhilaration and the terrors of sociocultural change under the impact of new arrivals. It is not surprising that much of the emotional intensity of those challenges centres on the changing status of religious belief and cultural practice under conditions of secular modernity.

The sublime acted in some ways as an emblem of access to a transcendent realm, even if only as a site of yearning for an 'Absolute' into which singularity could be subsumed. Perhaps, after the sublime, wonder can come to represent the acceptance of a world without the Absolute, in which the startled recognition of difference can give rise to both challenge and shared delight.

Notes

1 Charles Taylor, *A Secular Age* (Cambridge, MA: Harvard University Press, 2008). See especially, Part IV, 'Narratives of Secularisation', pp. 423–538.
2 Taylor, *A Secular Age*, p. 255.
3 I am here following Frederick Beiser's useful demarcation in which 'German Idealism' is taken as generally referring to 'the tradition of philosophy from Kant to Hegel, and more specifically to the doctrines expounded by Kant, Fichte, Schelling, and Hegel, from roughly 1781 to 1801'; and 'Romantic Idealism' as a subset of those doctrines, centred on ideas of the Absolute, and especially of 'Absolute Ego' as a force able both to know and to produce Nature. See Frederick Beiser, 'Romantic Idealism', in Dalia Nasser, ed., *The Relevance of Romanticism: Essays on German Romantic Philosophy* (Oxford: Oxford University Press, 2014), p. 31.
4 G. W. F. Hegel, *Lectures on the History of Philosophy*, Vol. III, trans. E. S. Haldane and Frances H. Simson (London: Routledge and Kegan Paul, 1974), p. 481.

5 Hegel, *Lectures on the History of Philosophy*, p. 506.
6 Arthur O. Lovejoy, 'Schiller and the Genesis of German Romanticism', in *Essays in the History of Ideas* (Baltimore: The Johns Hopkins Press, 1948), p. 211.
7 Heidegger discusses the relations between Plato's treatment of the philosopher's access to knowledge of the Forms and the *Theaetetus* account of wonder, in a set of lectures of 1931–2, published as *Essence and Truth: Plato's Cave Analogy and Theaetetus*, trans. Ted Sadler (London: Continuum, 2002).
8 Jean-François Lyotard, *Lessons on the Analytic of the Sublime*, trans. Elizabeth Rottenberg (Stanford: Stanford University Press, 1994). Further page references will be given in the main text.
9 Kant, *Critique of Judgement*, Part I, Book II, Sec. 29, pp. 115–16.
10 Kant, *Critique of Judgement*, Part I, Book II, Sec. 29, pp. 124–5.
11 Kant, *Critique of Judgement*, Part I, Book II, p. 113.
12 David Hume, *An Inquiry Concerning the Principles of Morals*, ed. Charles W. Hendel (New York: The Liberal Arts Press, 1957), p. 80.
13 Kant, *Critique of Judgement*, Book II, Part I, Sec. 29, p. 128.
14 See especially Sadik J. Al-Azm, 'Islam and Secular Humanism', in *Is Islam Secularisable? Challenging Political and Religious Taboos* (Berlin: Gerlach Press, 2014), pp. 13–14.

Conclusion: The Future of Wonder

The sublime has become, in common parlance, a relatively tame affair. Its aura of intense emotion now hovers incongruously over things that in its prime would have been seen as too mundane to qualify for the epithet. As early as 1895, Thomas Paine observed, in *The Age of Reason*, that the sublime and the ridiculous were so nearly related that it was difficult to class them separately: one step above the sublime, makes the ridiculous; and one step above the ridiculous, makes the sublime again. The sublime – if it is supposed to mean much more than the very beautiful – no longer attracts serious theorising. Yet the idea of a form of wonder that reaches for the unattainable continues to fascinate and attract.

Kant sensibly acknowledged that his theorising of the sublime would not affect the way the Savoyard peasant responded to mountains. Yet, there are ways in which attending to how philosophers of the past construed particular emotions can illuminate changes in the emotions themselves. Understanding conceptual shifts in how they have been understood throughout intellectual history can yield valuable insights into broader social changes, and sometimes even influence those changes.

In his book *The Passions and the Interests*, Albert Hirschman addressed the conceptual shifts that helped make money-making pursuits come to be perceived as honourable, after being previously condemned or despised as vices of greed or avarice. His central theme was the marvellous metamorphosis of destructive 'passions' into 'virtues', via the intervening concept of the 'rational pursuit of interest'. He hoped that, through a better understanding of that episode in intellectual history, both critics and defenders of capitalism might perhaps improve their arguments. In concluding his own argument, he reflected: 'This is probably all one could ask of history, and of the history of ideas in particular: not to resolve issues, but to raise the level of the debate.'[1]

Philosophers have also discussed comparable transformations, in eighteenth-century contexts, of the understanding of the passion of pride. In his analyses in the *Ethics* of particular passions, Spinoza had treated pride as a character flaw – an excessive self-esteem, which makes us think more highly of ourselves than is just. For Hume, in contrast, pride was seen as a socially useful and agreeable passion, constructively strengthening the sense of self, and thereby encouraging the emulation of virtue. This contrast between Spinoza and Hume reflects the changing configurations of pride with other concepts: of selfhood; of the nature of emotions in general and their relations with reason and imagination; and of the processes through which social interaction shapes the assumptions and the aspirations of individual minds.[2]

It can be difficult to extricate philosophical disagreements about how emotions should be regarded from conceptual shifts that happen under the impact of social or cultural change. In the case of wonder, there are additional challenges. It can be difficult even to locate wonder, as an identifiable object for analysis, throughout the history of philosophical thought – not because it ceases to be experienced, but because at times it has no ready-made place in the flux and flow of mental states, conditions or dispositions. Wonder can, as we have seen, disappear from the cartography of 'passions', to be relocated as an elusive feature of the interplay between different faculties of the mind. Lacking any clear location, it sometimes seems to be grasped only in a sense of something that has gone missing.

In his *Lectures on the History of Philosophy*, Hegel warned against thinking of the history of philosophy as if it were a battlefield covered with the bones of the dead – a succession of refuted and spiritually dead systems, each of which has killed and buried the other. He himself thought of it, rather, as an unfolding of rational thought into 'spirit' – a progression in which there is a 'real connection' between the different developmental stages. We do not have to endorse Hegel's belief in the 'spirit of the world' to share his conviction that there is more to the history of philosophy than 'a mere collection of chance events, of expeditions of wandering knights, each going about fighting, struggling purposelessly, leaving no results to show for all his efforts'.[3]

Derrida has demonstrated the richness of informed readings of philosophical and literary texts of the past as a resource for understanding our present. Talking on a related topic – translation – he says, in the concluding sections of the first *Beast and Sovereign* seminar, that an 'interpretive' translation 'brings with it the whole of culture', and that such an exercise is 'not separable from histurial movements in which all the forces of the world and the age are engaged'; for the 'whole force of history' is at work in producing it.[4]

What Derrida here calls 'interpretive translation' is in important ways similar to his own strategy in offering close readings of literary and philosophical texts; and they are of course often interdependent exercises. Interpretive readings of the kind in which Derrida engaged demand extensive scholarship; that they are 'interpretive' does not mean that they are not 'objective'. It does, though, suggest that offering imaginative readings across time of literary and philosophical texts can be a more creative – and also more political – activity than it is commonly regarded.

In the case of wonder, we should not expect, in looking at its history, to find some definitively true theory of its nature or role that might be appropriated wholesale into our own present. Yet, in better understanding the expeditions of the old wanderers, we might find some insights which we can put to work. Wonder itself, after all, has often been thought of as the residue of the mind's own wandering, rather than as an arrival at certainty. We have seen moments in its history where earlier insights have been adapted or appropriated – for better or worse – to changing contexts: Burke and Kant on the 'sublime' of Longinus; Heidegger and Arendt on Socratic wonder; Derrida on old ideas of *aporia*. Whatever its hazards, it is an intellectual practice worthy of emulation.

There are examples in more recent philosophical writing of attempts to bring the philosophical history of wonder into contemporary contexts. In her book *Strange Wonder*, Mary-Jane Rubenstein has offered, among much else, a rearticulation of Heidegger's approach to wonder-at-the-ordinary.[5] She reconstructs wonder in response to the distrust sometimes directed at its supposed displacement by modern scientific methods. On Rubenstein's account, in our ambivalence about wonder we have come to think that, rather than enduring it, we should seek to cure or at least to tranquillise it. Modern thought, reluctant to accept the wondrous, has responded with a denial of its mystery, attempting to neutralise it with affirmations of assured knowledge. Wonder, accordingly, has become something to ration or rein in, to the detriment of the possibilities it offers for fruitful, engaged thinking.

Rubenstein's reconstruction of wonder aims to preserve the disturbing force of the mysterious within the everyday, though without endorsing Heidegger's own disturbing talk of a sustained 'withdrawal' into the contemplation of that mystery. A revitalised Heideggerian approach brings a welcome emphasis on a thoughtful, questioning cast of mind, directed to the 'ordinary'. It also, though, may seem to suggest a sharper distinction than is appropriate between philosophical thought – inspired by wonder – and the desire for scientific explanation. Should the thought patterns of modern science be so sharply contrasted with a philosophical style of thinking which claims a distinctive connection with the wonder extolled by the ancient Greeks?

Taking a different perspective, Philip Fisher, in his book *Wonder, the Rainbow and the Aesthetics of Rare Experiences*, has argued for a reconnection of modern science with ancient ideas of wonder, and for a related rethinking of the relations between science and aesthetics. As an adaptation and expansion of the old dictum that philosophy – broadly construed as theoretical inquiry – begins in wonder, he suggests instead that it 'begins in wonder, continues on at every moment by means of wonder, and ends with explanation that produces, when first heard, a new and equally powerful experience of wonder to that with which it began'.[6]

Fisher describes the version of wonder captured in that formulation as 'the poetics of thought'. While retaining wonder's connections with theoretical inquiry, his expansion of the concept relocates its presence to the whole process of coming to know. No longer confined to the beginnings of inquiry, or left behind by explanation, wonder is here seen as pervading the whole movement of thought to its completion, where it begins again. Wonder, rather than being associated with unsatisfied desire, persists as ongoing pleasure in knowledge.

Thus construed, contemporary wonder need not be exclusively appropriated by any self-styled 'philosophical' form of thinking. Something is retained of the old idea of wonder as the beginnings of theoretical inquiry, without restricting its proper place to any particular way of conducting that inquiry. It can be appropriated by science, no less than by what we now recognise as academic philosophy.

The role of wonder in relation to contemporary ethical themes is harder to disentangle from broader treatments of imagination in conjunction with emotion. However, in a thoughtful and thought-provoking book, *Wonder and Generosity*, Marguerite La Caze has argued for its importance in shaping responses to a wide range of current social issues, including the treatment of refugees and asylum seekers, and the redressing of historical injustices towards indigenous peoples. La Caze's approach draws on Descartes' treatment of wonder in the *Passions of the Soul* – as read by Luce Irigaray.

In a section of *An Ethics of Sexual Difference*, originally published in 1984, Irigaray offered an imaginative reading of Descartes.[7] She argued that wonder – the passion which Descartes treated as 'the first of the passions' – is indeed indispensable, both to human life in general and to the creation of an ethics 'of and through sexual difference'. On her account, sexual difference is a prime occasion for the recognition of what is 'other', and hence a significant site of wonder: 'This other, male or female, should *surprise* us again and again, appear to us as *new, very different* from what we knew or what we thought he or she should be' (p. 107).

Irigaray's reading highlights Descartes' claim that wonder – unlike his other 'primary' passions – arises prior to the evaluation of its objects as good or bad. On her analysis, this suggests that wonder excludes any effort to assimilate its object or reduce it to sameness. The state of wonder rests with the recognition of difference. As the soul's sudden surprise, it is 'the moment of illumination – already and still contemplative – between the subject and the world' (p. 109). It is thus 'the passion of the first encounter', belonging 'outside repetition' (p. 113).

Drawing on that positive reading of the element of surprise in Cartesian wonder, La Caze argues, persuasively, that the ethical significance of wonder can be best developed by bringing its emphasis on difference into interaction with other emotions. It is important especially, she suggests, in its interactions with an emotion which seems initially at odds with it – the passion that Descartes called *generosité:* the recognition of commonalities between human beings, which undermines inappropriate feelings of superiority.

For Descartes, *generosité* centres on a sense of rightful self-esteem, which demands equally a respect for others. Its resistance to excessive self-esteem is based on recognition of a shared human capacity for free choice, which he construed in terms of the exercise of a virtuous will. Stressing the potential for reciprocal respect in this analysis, La Caze argues that, although they may initially seem opposed, wonder and this form of generosity together yield a kind of ethical thinking in which both commonality and otherness are acknowledged and embraced. Wonder, in this configuration, involves an openness towards others, in appreciative recognition of their difference from ourselves.

It is an approach that accentuates wonder's traditional strong orientation towards attitudes of admiration and awe. In an interesting discussion of issues related to genocide and collective forgiveness, La Caze argues that these associations can make wonder an unacceptable response to acts of extreme evil.[8] Radical evil, she observes, poses challenges for understanding both wonder and generosity; for evil demands judgement, and stretches the limits of our respect for others.

It is an intriguing argument. Surprised and puzzled though we might be in the face of the perpetration of extreme evil, that bewilderment is indeed a response very different from the experience of admiring awe described in Descartes' treatment of wonder. Can we – should we – wonder at evil? Or should the compass of wonder be restricted to what is appropriately apprehended with admiring awe? There are echoes in La Caze's argumentation of Descartes' own cautions about wonder, though she is concerned with ways in which wonder can inhibit moral judgement, rather than with its stupefying effects on theoretical inquiry. If we bring Spinoza into the picture, we may see its effects on judgement in a different light: wonder can be an energising impulse towards greater reflective engagement, rather than the onset of a harmful paralysis. Wonder can be associated with dismay, as well as with admiring awe.

Whatever we conclude on that issue, the consideration of wonder in its interactions with other emotions opens up rich possibilities for understanding its place in our lives, and the circumstances in which we might or might not want to celebrate its role – whether as admiring awe or as dismayed indignation. Here again, as we have seen in relation to a range of moments in the philosophical history of wonder, there may be no final truth of the matter. Yet reconnecting with these past philosophical reflections on wonder can enrich debate – even where there is no definitive conclusion to be reached.

The exercise of 'reclaiming' wonder which this book has addressed has had two main concerns. First, to establish points of connection with past philosophical thinking which might bring a renewed appreciation of the nature and significance of wonder. Second, to challenge the ways in which a particular form of wonder has come to dominate our understanding of it and our attitudes towards it. I have tried to argue a case for reclaiming the rich variety of wonder, which has been largely subsumed into the mesmerising force of one of its versions: the Romantic understanding of the sublime, which had its context in post-Kantian ideas of the Absolute.

That version of wonder had its own noble sublimity. There was a certain grandeur in its aspirations, and something that elicits admiration and awe in its efforts to break through the limits of the 'ordinary'. Yet its surviving remnants – shorn of the sustaining power of the Absolute which framed it – eclipse the richness of what wonder has been in the past, and what it might yet be.

Even if we do not accept a redescription of wonder as the 'poetics' of scientific thought, we can recognise its continuing role in the pursuit of adequate explanation. Whatever threats it may have seemed to pose in the past, wonder can now be readily acknowledged as a source of strength in sustaining intellectual activity, enhancing its power and adding motivational force to its rigours. Wonder can drive us on to seek ever better scientific explanations. Yet the pause it induces in thinking can also turn us towards alternative modes of inquiry or ways of thinking. We wonder *whether*, as in our tentative testing of a scientific hypothesis; but we can also wonder *at* something we come to see as strange or unfamiliar, which had previously seemed commonplace. Not all efforts to understand find their proper satisfaction in complete explanations of the natures of things. Rather than making us demand explanations, our wonder might express a desire for a subtler, more nuanced articulation of the strangeness of what confronts us. It might direct us from science to art or literature – or philosophy – and back again.

Maurice Merleau-Ponty, in the Preface to his *Phenomenology of Perception*, talked of a sense of mystery about the world and about reason, which cannot be dispelled by finding some 'solution'. He was talking about the phenomenological approach to philosophy, which he saw as demanding the same kind of painstaking attentiveness, and openness to wonder, that is to be expected from literature – a cast of mind which merges into 'the general effort of modern thought'.[9] Merleau-Ponty had in mind, especially, the orientation of phenomenology towards the description of experience. However, it is a point which need not be restricted to one style of philosophical thinking – or to philosophy as a specific kind of thinking.

Wonder depends on strangeness; yet it can seem such a familiar experience that it barely warrants investigation. On closer examination, it is something rich and strange. As a topic, it fits much of its own definition – something familiar, but barely understood, which draws our imagination on and engages our emotions.

My discussions of wonder in this book have highlighted one of its less obvious features: the ways in which it challenges ideals centred on certainty. Wonder, in its many forms, has provided an intellectual space – a temporary pause – which fosters the renewal of active, imaginative, emotionally engaged thinking. It depends but also thrives on the absence of certainty. It has often been associated with explicitly celebrated forms of 'not-knowing', which can make wonder suspect in the many contemporary contexts where certainty is extolled as a value – even as a universal human need. Understanding wonder better can alert us to the contingency, and the inadequacies, of that privileging of certainty.

Wonder's long connections with uncertainty may assist the exercise of judgement in one area of current debate where many of the issues addressed in this book converge: the human contribution to global warming. Exultant celebration of the powers of human reason has been part of the legacy of the sublime. The Kantian vision of a noble struggle between rival faculties of the mind – reaching a balance in 'discordant concord' – fitted well with the understanding of human beings as representing the highest reaches of species development, within a world whose rational order was assured. The place of humanity within the rest of nature shared that aura of harmonising grandeur. The internal harmonising of forces within the mind could be projected onto a benign view of humanity as a positive presence in the world. It is a vision that barely makes sense in a context where the powers of human reason have come to be seen as complicit in the disintegration of the established 'order of Nature'.

We have seen that elements of Spinoza's philosophy were appropriated – along with Kantian themes – into the Romantic Idealism which nurtured the idea of the sublime. It is striking, then, that Spinoza can also be read now as having had prescient glimpses into the future unravelling of that exultation in the sublimity of human reason. There are tensions within his treatment in the *Ethics* of the correspondence between mind and matter. On the one hand, there are the relations between parallel, rationally ordered totalities of ideas and of things. On the other, at the level of the individual mind, we are in the confused realm of inadequate ideas – the realm of Imagination. On the one hand, we are assured that the whole of reality is, in principle, accessible to the mind's rationally ordered adequate ideas. On the other, the very existence of an individual mind resides in its ongoing struggle to sustain what limited clarity it can attain, immersed as it is within that totality of being. To understand the *Ethics*, we must move between the intellectual apprehension of the totality and consideration of our own unavoidably limited perspectives within it all – between two ways of thinking of the powers and limitations of human reason.

In Chapter 16 of the *Theological-Political Treatise*, however, Spinoza seems to see that tension in a different light. There, he offers a startling observation on the fragile place of human reason within the whole of Nature. Nature, he says, is not bounded by the laws of human reason, which aim only at human well-being and preservation. Nature's limits are infinitely wider, referring to an eternal order; and, in that infinite order, human reason itself is just a speck. He goes on to warn that we should not then expect things to be arranged according to what our reason dictates.

At first sight, the point here is relatively straightforward: from our limited position within the whole, we cannot presume to judge what is good or bad for the order of things in their entirety. Yet Spinoza goes further, appearing to suggest that the laws of our reason simply do not apply to the whole of nature. It seems clear, at any rate, that Spinoza's understanding of the human mind's place in Nature is a very long way indeed from Kant's exuberant celebration of its sublimity. Human reason, as it emerges in the *Theological-Political Treatise*, does not surpass – even with regard to its power of knowledge – the might of Nature.

Spinoza seems to glimpse the fragility and vulnerability of the very existence of human powers of reason, encompassed as they are by the cosmic enormity of the universe. There are of course limits to that insight. He was not able to contemplate the uncertainties we can now grasp about the future of human life as we know it – or about the future of life itself – under the catastrophic scenarios of global warming. Yet it does seem that he grasped something of the interconnectedness that underpins those scenarios. He did not know that life had emerged in a deep past, in which chance and catastrophe mingled with unimaginably slow adaptation. He had no knowledge of the extinction of species, which made possible the slow emergence of thinking beings capable of comprehending themselves as part of a world. He did not know that life is destined ultimately to disappear, in an unimaginably far future, from an earth whose conditions will no longer be able to sustain it.

Spinoza is now read in the light of contemporary knowledge of deep time, in the light of Darwin, and in the light of more recent developments in evolutionary biology. Yet his insights resonate with ways of thinking which he could not himself have envisaged – beyond exultation in human reason as the locus of the Romantic sublime. His insistence that human beings be seen as part of nature reverberates in contemporary notions of human life as interconnected with broader complex and fragile eco-systems. Much of that understanding is at odds with older ideas of humanity as the paramount species – as life's highest achievement, the apex of the natural order, shaping 'its' world from that superior position.

We can now grasp the real possibility that the conditions for life to flourish are diminishing. We face the prospect that the earth may cease to sustain human flourishing – not just, inevitably, in a deep future, but under more imminent conditions, brought about contingently by the very capacities that made human beings distinctive. Older affirmations of awe at distinctively human powers are now counter-poised to apprehension about the fragility of life itself in the world they have shaped.

Kantian awe at the starry skies above is no longer readily juxtaposed with self-congratulation about the grandeur of the operations of the human mind within. Yet wonder is intensified, rather than weakened, by increased understanding of just how tiny that human speck is in relation to the immensity beyond. Our own times are seeing a growing popular interest in astronomy and cosmology. That strengthening of wonder at the immensity of the universe comes at a time of increased awareness of the fragility of life under changing conditions.

Wonder at the immensity of the universe can bring a sharper sense of the fragility of what is near. It may be a fortuitous conjunction; yet it is also a felicitous one. Intensified wonder – stimulating increased understanding – may yet bring political insight. Meanwhile, it should be no surprise that debates about climate change are subject to the same volatile mix of clashing 'certainties', perverse varieties of scepticism, and competing accusations of stupidity that afflict current debates on that other great challenge of our times with which it is increasingly interconnected: the mass movements of people.

Wonder has been seen both as a stupefaction and as a revitalising response to mental inertia. Its apparent contradictions are part of its strangeness. The explicit linking of wonder with a form of stupidity may seem to be among the more outlandish moments in its variegated history. I have tried, nonetheless, to show what made those connections plausible, and to illustrate how an understanding of wonder can yield insight into our own contemporary vulnerability to - and complicity in – the operations of collective stupidity.

In *Middlemarch*, George Eliot has her narrator observe: 'If we had a keen vision and feeling of all ordinary human life, it would be like hearing the grass grow and the squirrel's heart beat, and we should die of that roar which lies on the other side of silence. As it is, the quickest of us walk about well wadded with stupidity.'[10] It is of course an ironic authorial voice. Eliot is not really celebrating stupidity, or deriding artistic vision. She is acknowledging the inevitability of the self-protective insensibility which allows her readers to continue to walk around their human world without being constantly overwhelmed. Yet she is also celebrating – and enacting – the artist's 'keen vision and feeling' through which the tragedies of the ordinary become visible.

Eliot is here, as often, moving cleverly between different perspectives – between artistic vision and blunted, everyday apprehension of the 'ordinary' – which she then transforms by bringing artistic vision to bear on it. There is generosity, as well as ironic self-mockery, in her contrast: we cannot always be vigilant to catch the beating of the squirrel's heart; and it is well that we do not always feel the intensity of the emotion that surrounds us. A perpetually keen artistic vision would make living impossible. Yet there is a sting in the authorial observation. Collective stupidity sustains us amidst the unavoidable demands of daily life; yet it is stupidity, nonetheless.

It is no accident that the piercing delights of wonder are intermingled with the numbing effects of stupidity. Heidegger insisted that anything at all can become – in its usualness – an object of wonder. Yet it is a condition which, of its nature, cannot be sustained for everything all of the time. Perhaps, at any rate, a better understanding of its past can sharpen our vision, help protect us from some collective obfuscations, and sustain our hopes of where wandering wonder might lead us in the future.

Notes

1. Albert O. Hirschman, *The Passions and the Interests: Political Arguments for Capitalism Before its Triumph* (Princeton: Princeton University Press, 1977), p. 135.
2. For a helpful discussion of Hume's role in those changes, see Jacqueline A. Taylor, *Reflecting Subjects: Passion, Sympathy, and Society in Hume's Philosophy* (Oxford: Oxford University Press, 2015), especially Chapter 5, 'The Dangers and Dignity of Pride'.
3. G. W. F. Hegel, *Lectures on the History of Philosophy*, Vol. I, trans. E. S. Haldane and Frances H. Simson (London: Routledge and Kegan Paul, 1974), p. 19.
4. Derrida, *The Beast and the Sovereign*, Vol. I, p. 338.
5. Mary-Jane Rubenstein, *Strange Wonder: The Closure of Metaphysics and the Opening of Awe* (New York: Columbia University Press, 2008).
6. Philip Fisher, *Wonder, the Rainbow, and the Aesthetics of Rare Experiences* (Cambridge, MA: Harvard University Press, 1998), p. 41.
7. Luce Irigaray, 'Wonder: A Reading of Descartes' *The Passions of the Soul*', in Susan Bordo, ed., *Feminist Interpretations of René Descartes* (University Park: Pennsylvania University Press, 1999), pp. 105–13. Originally from *An Ethics of Sexual Difference*, trans. Carolyn Burke and Gillian C. Gill (Ithaca: Cornell University Press, 1993). Further page references to the Bordo edition will be given in the main text.
8. Marguerite La Caze, *Wonder and Generosity: Their Role in Ethics and Politics* (Albany: State University of New York Press, 2013), Chapter 6, 'Wonder, Radical Evil, and Forgiveness'.
9. Maurice Merleau-Ponty, *Phenomenology of Perception*, trans. Colin Smith (London: Routledge & Kegan Paul, 1962), pp. xx-xxi.
10. George Eliot, *Middlemarch: A Study of Provincial Life* (London: Oxford University Press, 1947), Ch. XX, p. 207.

Bibliography

Agacinski, Sylviane, 'We Are Not Sublime: Love and Sacrifice, Abraham and Ourselves', in Jonathan Rée and Jane Chamberlain, eds, *Kierkegaard: A Critical Reader* (Oxford: Blackwell, 1998), pp. 129–51.

Agamben, Giorgio, 'Beyond Human Rights', in Paolo Virno and Michael Hardt, eds, *Radical Thought in Italy: A Potential Politics* (Minneapolis: University of Minnesota Press, 1996).

Agamben, Giorgio, *Means Without End: Notes on Politics* (Theory Out of Bounds, Vol. 20) (Minneapolis and London: University of Minnesota Press, 2000).

Al-Azm, Sadik J., *Is Islam Secularisable? Challenging Political and Religious Taboos* (Berlin: Gerlach Press, 2014).

Aquinas, St Thomas, *Summa Theologiae* [1265–74], second and revised edition (1920), literally translated by Fathers of the English Dominican Province (Coyote Canyon Press, 2010), online edition.

Arendt, Hannah, *The Human Condition* (New York: Doubleday Anchor, 1959).

Arendt, Hannah, *The Life of the Mind* (New York and London: Harcourt Brace Jovanovich, 1971).

Arendt, Hannah, 'Martin Heidegger at Eighty', *New York Review of Books*, 21 October 1971.

Arendt, Hannah, *The Origins of Totalitarianism* (New York: Harcourt Brace Jovanovich, 1973).

Arendt, Hannah, *Lectures on Kant's Political Philosophy*, ed. Ronald Beiner (Chicago: University of Chicago Press, 1982).

Arendt, Hannah, 'We Refugees', in Marc Robinson, ed., *Altogether Elsewhere: Writers in Exile* (Boston: Faber & Faber, 1994), pp. 110–19.

Arendt, Hannah, *On Revolution* [1963] (London: Penguin Books, 2006).

BIBLIOGRAPHY

Aristotle, *Metaphysics*, trans. W. D. Ross, in Richard McKeon, ed., *The Basic Works of Aristotle* (New York: Random House, 1941), pp. 682–926.

Aristotle, *Rhetoric*, trans. W. Rhys Roberts, in Richard McKeon, ed., *The Basic Works of Aristotle* (New York: Random House, 1941), pp. 1318–431.

Beiser, Frederick, 'Kant's Intellectual Development: 1746–1781', in Paul Guyer, ed., *The Cambridge Companion to Kant* (Cambridge: Cambridge University Press, 1992), pp. 26–61.

Beiser, Frederick, 'Romanticism and Idealism', in Dalia Nassar, ed., *The Relevance of Romanticism: Essays on German Romantic Philosophy* (Oxford: Oxford University Press, 2014), pp. 30–45.

Benitez, Eugenio and Guimaraes, Livia, 'Philosophy as Performed in Plato's *Theaetetus*', *Review of Metaphysics,* Vol. XLVII, No. 2, 1993, pp. 297–328.

Blanchot, Maurice, *The Writing of the Disaster*, trans. Ann Smock (Lincoln and London: University of Nebraska Press, 1995).

Blanchot, Maurice, *The Instant of My Death*, with Jacques Derrida, *Demeure: Fiction and Testimony*, trans. Elizabeth Rottenberg (Stanford: Stanford University Press, 2000).

Bottici, Chiara, *Imaginal Politics: Images Beyond Imagination and the Imaginary* (New York: Columbia University Press, 2014).

Bourke, Richard, *Empire and Revolution: The Political Life of Edmund Burke* (Princeton: Princeton University Press, 2015).

Bromwich, David, *Moral Imagination: Essays* (Princeton: Princeton University Press, 2014).

Bromwich, David, *The Intellectual Life of Edmund Burke: From the Sublime and Beautiful to American Independence* (Cambridge, MA: Harvard University Press, 2014).

Brown, Deborah, *Descartes and the Passionate Mind* (Cambridge: Cambridge University Press, 2006).

Burke, Edmund, *Collected Works* (Minerva Classics, 2013), Kindle edition.

Burke, Edmund, *A Philosophical Enquiry into the Sublime and Beautiful* [1757], ed. Paul Guyer, (Oxford: Oxford University Press, 2015).

Burnyeat, Myles, ed., *The Theaetetus of Plato* (Indianapolis: Hackett Publishing Company, 1990).

Castoriadis, Cornelius, 'Radical Imagination and the Social Instituting Imaginary', in Gillian Robinson and John Rundell, eds, *Rethinking Imagination* (London and New York: Routledge, 1994), pp. 136–54.

Culler, Jonathan, *Flaubert: The Uses of Uncertainty* (Aurora, CO: Davies Group, 1984).

Daston, Lorraine and Katharine Park, *Wonders and the Order of Nature, 1150–1750* (New York: Zone Books, 2001).

Deleuze, Gilles, *Kant's Critical Philosophy: The Doctrine of the Faculties* (Minneapolis: University of Minnesota Press, 1984).
Deleuze, Gilles, *Difference and Repetition*, trans. Paul Patton (New York: Columbia University Press, 1994).
Derrida, Jacques, *Memoires for Paul de Man*, revised edition, trans. Cecile Lindsay, Jonathan Culler, Eduardo Cadava and Peggy Kamuf (New York: Columbia University Press, 1989).
Derrida, Jacques, *Aporias*, trans. Thomas Dutot (Stanford: Stanford University Press, 1993).
Derrida, Jacques, *Demeure: Fiction and Testimony*, with Maurice Blanchot, *The Instant of My Death*, trans. Elizabeth Rottenberg (Stanford: Stanford University Press, 1998).
Derrida, Jacques, 'An Idea of Flaubert: "Plato's Letter"', in *Psyche: Inventions of the Other*, ed. Peggy Kamuf and Elizabeth Rottenberg (Stanford: Stanford University Press, 2007), pp. 299-317.
Derrida, Jacques, *The Gift of Death*, second edition, and *Literature in Secret*, trans. David Wills (Chicago and London: University of Chicago Press, 2008).
Derrida, Jacques, *The Beast and the Sovereign*, Vol. I, ed. Geoffrey Bennington and Peggy Kamuf (Chicago: University of Chicago Press, 2009).
Derrida, Jacques, *The Beast and the Sovereign*, Vol. II, ed. Michael Lisse, Marie-Louise Mallet and Ginette Michaud, trans. Geoffrey Bennington (Chicago: University of Chicago Press, 2011).
Descartes, René, *The Passions of the Soul*, in John Cottingham, Robert Stoothoff and Dugald Murdoch, ed. and trans., *The Philosophical Writings of Descartes*, Vol. I (Cambridge: Cambridge University Press, 1985), pp. 325–404.
Deutscher, Max, *Judgment After Arendt* (Aldershot: Ashgate, 2007).
Eliot, George, *Middlemarch: A Study of Provincial Life* (London: Oxford University Press, 1947).
Fisher, Philip, *Wonder, the Rainbow, and the Aesthetics of Rare Experiences* (Cambridge, MA: Harvard University Press, 1998).
Flaubert, Gustave, *The Letters of Gustave Flaubert 1830–1857*, selected, ed. and trans. Francis Steegmuller (London: Faber and Faber, 1980).
Flaubert, Gustave, *The Correspondence of Gustave Flaubert and George Sand*, trans. Francis Steegmuller and Barbara Bray (London: Harvill Press, 1999).
Flaubert, Gustave, *The Temptation of St Anthony* [1874], trans. Lafcadio Hearn (New York: Random House, Modern Library Paperback, 2001).
Flaubert, Gustave, *Bouvard and Pecuchet* [1881], trans. Mark Polizzotti (Dalkey Archive Press, 2005).

Flaubert, Gustave, *Madame Bovary* [1857], trans. Adam Thorpe (London: Vintage Books, 2012).

Flaubert, Gustave, 'Bibliomania' [1837], trans. Andrew Brown, in *Memoirs of a Madman and November* (Richmond: Alma Classics, 2013), pp. 61–76.

Foucault, Michel, 'Fantasies of the Library', in *Language, Counter-Memory, Practice: Selected Essays and Interviews*, ed. Donald F. Boucher (Ithaca: Cornell University Press, 1977), pp. 87–112.

Hargraves, Orin, *It's Been Said Before: A Guide to the Use and Abuse of Clichés* (Oxford: Oxford University Press, 2014).

Hari, Johann, *Chasing the Scream: The First and Last Days of the War on Drugs* (New York: Bloomsbury, 2005).

Hegel, G. W. F., *Lectures on the History of Philosophy*, trans. E. S. Haldane and Frances H. Simson (London: Routledge and Kegan Paul, 1974), Vols I and III.

Hegel, G. W. F., *Phenomenology of Spirit* [1807], trans. A. V. Miller (Oxford: Oxford University Press, 1977).

Heidegger, Martin, *Being and Time*, trans. John Macquarrie and Edward Robinson (Oxford: Basil Blackwell, 1962).

Heidegger, Martin, *Nietzsche, Vol. III: The Will to Power as Knowledge and as Metaphysics*, ed. David Farrell Krell (San Francisco: Harper Collins, 1991).

Heidegger, Martin, *Basic Questions of Philosophy: Selected Problems of Logic*, trans. Richard Rojcewicz and André Schuwer (Bloomington and Indianapolis: Indiana University Press, 1994).

Heidegger, Martin, *The Fundamental Concepts of Metaphysics: World, Finitude, Solitude*, trans. William McNeill and Nicholas Walker (Bloomington and Minneapolis: Indiana University Press, 1995).

Heidegger, Martin, *Essence and Truth: Plato's Cave Allegory and Theaetetus*, trans. Ted Sadler (London: Continuum, 2002).

Hirschman, Albert O., *The Passions and the Interests: Political Arguments for Capitalism Before its Triumph* (Princeton: Princeton University Press, 1977).

Hume, David, *An Inquiry Concerning the Principles of Morals* [1752], ed. Charles W. Hendel (New York: The Liberal Arts Press, 1957).

Hume, David, *A Treatise of Human Nature* [1739], ed. L. A. Selby-Bigge (Oxford: Oxford University Press, 1978).

Hume, David, 'Of the Standard of Taste', in *Selected Essays*, ed. Stephen Copley and Andrew Edgar (Oxford: Oxford University Press, 1993), pp. 133–54.

Huntington, Samuel P., *The Clash of Civilisations and the Remaking of the World Order* (New York: Simon and Schuster, 1997).

Irigaray, Luce, 'Wonder: A Reading of Descartes' *The Passions of the Soul*', trans. Carolyn Burke and Gillian C. Gill, in Susan Bordo, ed., *Feminist Interpretations of René Descartes* (University Park: Pennsylvania University Press, 1999), pp. 105–13; reprinted from *An Ethics of Sexual Difference* (Ithaca: Cornell University Press, 1993).

James, Susan, *Passion and Action: The Emotions in Seventeenth-Century Philosophy* (Oxford: Clarendon Press, 1997).

James, Susan, *Spinoza on Philosophy, Religion, and Politics: The Theological-Political Treatise* (Oxford: Oxford University Press, 2012).

Kant, Immanuel, *The Critique of Judgement* [1790], trans. James Creed Meredith (Oxford: Clarendon Press, 1952).

Kant, Immanuel, *Critique of Practical Reason* [1788], trans. Lewis White Beck (New York: The Liberal Arts Press, 1956).

Kant, Immanuel, *Critique of Pure Reason* [1781], trans. Norman Kemp Smith (London: Macmillan, 1956).

Kant, Immanuel, *Observations on the Feeling of the Beautiful and the Sublime* [1764], trans. John T. Goldthwait (Berkeley and Los Angeles: University of California Press, 1960).

Kant, Immanuel, *Political Writings*, ed. Hans Reiss, trans. H. B. Nisbet (Cambridge: Cambridge University Press, 1991).

Kompridis, N., ed, *Philosophical Romanticism* (London and New York: Routledge, 2006).

Kundnani, Arun, *The Muslims Are Coming: Islamophobia, Extremism, and the Domestic War on Terror* (London and New York: Verso, 2014).

La Caze, Marguerite, *Wonder and Generosity: Their Role in Ethics and Politics* (Albany: State University of New York Press, 2013).

Lambert, Gregg, *Return Statements: The Return of Religion in Contemporary Philosophy* (Edinburgh: Edinburgh University Press, 2016).

Lloyd, Genevieve, *Part of Nature: Self-Knowledge in Spinoza's Ethics* (Ithaca and London: Cornell University Press, 1994).

Lloyd, Genevieve, *Spinoza and the Ethics* (London and New York: Routledge, 1996).

Lloyd, Genevieve, 'Hume on the Passion for Truth', in Anne Jaap Jacobson, ed., *Feminist Interpretations of David Hume* (University Park: Pennsylvania State University Press, 2000), pp. 39–59.

Lloyd, Genevieve, *Enlightenment Shadows* (Oxford: Oxford University Press, 2013).

Lloyd, Genevieve, *Spinoza and the Idea of the Secular* (Mededelingen Vanwege Het Spinozahuis, No. 102) (Voorschoten: Uitgeverij Spinozahuis, 2013).

Lloyd, Genevieve, 'The Philosophical History of Wonder', *Graduate Faculty Philosophy Journal*, Vol. 34, No. 2, 2013, pp. 299–316.

Lloyd, Genevieve, 'Nomadic Subjects and Asylum Seekers', in Bolette Blaagaard and Iris van der Tuin, eds, *The Subject of Rosi Braidotti: Politics and Concepts* (London: Bloomsbury, 2014), pp. 185–9.

Lloyd, Genevieve, 'Derrida and the Philosophical History of Wonder', *Parrhesia*, No. 24, 2015, pp. 64–82.

Lloyd, Genevieve and Moira Gatens, *Collective Imaginings: Spinoza, Past and Present* (London and New York: Routledge, 1999).

Lovejoy, Arthur O., 'Schiller and the Genesis of German Romanticism', in *Essays in the History of Ideas* (Baltimore: The Johns Hopkins Press, 1948), pp. 207–27.

Lyotard, Jean-François, *Lessons on the Analytic of the Sublime*, trans. Elizabeth Rottenberg (Stanford: Stanford University Press, 1994).

Malpas, Jeff, 'Beginning in Wonder: Placing the Origin of Thinking', in N. Kompridis, ed., *Philosophical Romanticism* (London and New York: Routledge, 2006), pp. 282–98.

Merleau-Ponty, Maurice, *Phenomenology of Perception*, trans. Colin Smith (London: Routledge and Kegan Paul, 1962).

Nasser, Dalia, ed., *The Relevance of Romanticism: Essays on German Romantic Philosophy* (Oxford: Oxford University Press, 2014).

Novalis [Friedrich von Hardenberg], *Philosophical Writings*, ed. and trans. Margaret Mahony Stoljar (Albany: State University of New York Press, 1997).

Orwell, George, 'Politics and the English Language', in *A Collection of Essays* (Orlando: Harcourt Books, 1981).

Plato, *Apology*, trans. F. J. Church, in *The Trial and Death of Socrates* (London: Macmillan, 1952), pp. 33–78.

Plato, *Symposium*, trans. Benjamin Jowett, in *The Dialogues of Plato*, Vol. 2 (London: Sphere Books, 1970), pp. 179–238.

Plato, *Republic*, trans. A. D. Lindsay (London: J. M. Dent & Sons, 1976).

Plato, *Theaetetus*, trans. Margaret Jane Levett, in Myles Burnyeat, ed., *The Theaetetus of Plato* (Indianapolis: Hackett, 1990).

Ronell, Avital, *Stupidity* (Urbana and Chicago: University of Illinois Press, 2002).

Rosenthal, Michael A., 'Miracles, Wonder, and the State', in Yitzhak Y. Melamed and Michael A. Rosenthal, eds, *Spinoza's Theological-Political Treatise: A Critical Guide* (Cambridge: Cambridge University Press), pp. 231–49.

Rousseau, Jean-Jacques, *A Discourse on the Moral Effects of the Arts and Sciences* [1750], in *The Social Contract and Discourses*, trans. G. D. H. Cole (London: J. M. Dent & Sons, 1975).

Rousseau, Jean-Jacques, *A Discourse on the Origin of Inequality* [1754], in *The Social Contract and Discourses*, trans. G. D. H. Cole (London: J. M. Dent & Sons, 1975).

Rubenstein, Mary-Jane, *Strange Wonder: The Closure of Metaphysics and the Opening of Awe* (New York: Columbia University Press, 2008).

Rubenstein, Mary-Jane, 'Heidegger's Caves: On Dwelling in Wonder', in Sophia Vasalou, ed., *Practices of Wonder: Cross-Disciplinary Perspectives* (Eugene: Wipf and Stock, 2012), pp. 144–65.

Sartre, Jean-Paul, *The Family Idiot: Gustave Flaubert 1821–1857*, Vol. I, trans. Carol Cosman (Chicago: University of Chicago Press, 1951).

Schopenhauer, Arthur, *The World as Will and Representation* [1819], Vol. I of The Cambridge Edition of the Works of Schopenhauer, ed. and trans. Judith Norman, Alistair Welchman and Christopher Janaway (Cambridge: Cambridge University Press, 2010).

Shelley, Mary, *Frankenstein or The Modern Prometheus: The 1818 Text*, ed. Marilyn Butler (Oxford: Oxford University Press, 2008).

Solomon, Robert C. and Kathleen M. Higgins, eds, *The Age of German Idealism*, Routledge History of Philosophy, Vol. VI (London and New York: Routledge, 1993).

Spinoza, Benedict de, *Ethics* [1677], in Edwin Curley, ed. and trans., *The Collected Works of Spinoza*, Vol. I (Princeton: Princeton University Press, 1985).

Spinoza, Benedict de, *Theological-Political Treatise* [1670], in Edwin Curley, ed. and trans., *The Collected Works of Spinoza*, Vol. II (Princeton: Princeton University Press, 2016).

Stone, I. F., *The Trial and Death of Socrates* (London: Pimlico, 1988).

Taylor, Charles, *Modern Social Imaginaries* (Durham, NC: Duke University Press, 2004).

Taylor, Charles, *A Secular Age* (Cambridge, MA: Harvard University Press, 2008).

Taylor, Jacqueline A., *Reflecting Subjects: Passion, Sympathy, and Society in Hume's Philosophy* (Oxford: Oxford University Press, 1977).

Vasalou, Sophia, *Wonder: A Grammar* (Albany: SUNY Press, 2016).

Wittgenstein, Ludwig, *Lecture on Ethics*, ed. Edoardo Zamuner, Ermelinda Valentina Di Lascio and D. K. Levy (Chichester: John Wiley and Sons, 2014).

Index

Absolute, the, 187–91, 196–7, 203, 203n3, 213
admiration, 45, 52, 57, 128, 135, 213
Agacinski, Sylviane, 88–90, 199
Al-Azm, Sadik J., 202
aporia, 127–30, 139, 140–5, 157, 164, 208
Aquinas, St Thomas, 26–7, 39
Arendt, Hannah, 132–9, 165–70, 175–6, 180, 181, 192, 208
Aristotle, 24–30, 32–6, 39, 54
art, 94, 108
astonishment, 33–4, 55–60, 126–9, 133, 146; *see also* surprise
asylum seekers *see* refugees
attunement, 121–5, 131
Augustine, St, 201
awe, 126–7, 183, 200, 212, 213

Beiser, Frederick, 203n3
bêtise see stupidity
Blanchot, Maurice, 147–8
boredom, 123–5

Bottici, Chiara, 159–63
Burke, Edmund, 52–63, 67, 156, 164–5, 208

cabinets of wonder, 36, 131
Castoriadis, Cornelius, 158
certainty, 17, 21, 28, 48, 78, 106, 110–12, 122–3, 136, 175–8, 188, 201, 214–15, 218
clichés, 95–6, 106, 142, 155–6, 160, 163–4, 178
climate change, 218
Colet, Louise, 92
compassion, 178–81
conatus, 39, 43, 73–5
critique, social, 18–19, 23, 139, 157–8, 161, 164–5
crowds, 60, 61–2, 96–7
curiosity, 35, 55–7, 78, 130

Daston, Lorraine, 36
De Man, Paul, 141
death
   Derrida on, 143, 145–9
   in *Frankenstein,* 82, 84–5

Heidegger on, 125–6
in *Madame Bovary*, 98–9
Plato on, 18, 22–3
Spinoza on, 149
Deleuze, Gilles, 69–71, 149–50, 191, 193
Derrida, Jacques, 113, 140–53, 157, 164, 207–8
Descartes, René, 30–45, 49, 55, 59, 78, 122–3, 131, 136, 150, 152–3, 210–12
detachment, 58, 93, 96, 108, 131, 134, 136, 166–7, 180; *see also* objectivity
disdain, 42–3, 45

Eichmann, Adolf, 136
Eliot, George, 219–20
Elizabeth, Princess, 30
Enlightenment, the, 79, 103, 108, 112

Fichte, Johann, 188–9
Fisher, Philip, 209–10
Flaubert, Gustave, 92–118, 149–53, 154n17, 155–61
Foucault, Michel, 109–10

German Idealism *see* Idealism, German
Godwin, William, 79
grief, 98–9, 146–8

Hargraves, Orin, 163–4
Hegel, G. W. F., 74–5, 89, 188–90, 207

Heidegger, Martin, 120–32, 145, 208–9
Arendt on, 132–4, 166
Hirschman, Albert O., 205–6
Hume, David, 54, 56–7, 199, 206
Huntington, Samuel, 162

Idealism, German, 73–9, 187–91, 203n3; *see also* Romanticism
imaginary, social, 158–9; *see also* critique, social
imagination, 53, 56, 61, 86, 87, 159–60, 173, 181, 200
in Arendt, 137–9, 166
in Kant, 66–7, 70, 76, 120–1, 193–5
in Spinoza, 40–50, 158
Irigaray, Luce, 210–11

judgement, 104–5, 107, 155, 173, 176
aesthetic, 54, 78, 120, 186–7, 191–2
Arendt on, 134–9, 165–8, 192

Kant, Immanuel, 74–8, 137, 165–8, 187–8, 215, 218
on the sublime, 63–71, 191–200, 205
Kierkegaard, Søren, 88–90, 148–9

La Caze, Marguerite, 210–12
La Fontaine, Jean de, 144, 157

INDEX

Longinus, 54, 58, 63, 64, 89
Lovejoy, Arthur O., 189
Lyotard, Jean-François, 191–200

Merleau-Ponty, Maurice, 214
moral consciousness, 89–90, 185–7, 192

narratives
  Flaubert's strategies, 97–9, 104, 111
  in social critique, 155, 158, 164, 168, 173–6, 179
  in Spinoza, 46–9
Nietzsche, Friedrich, 77

objectivity, 54, 93, 96, 99, 138, 167, 181, 186–7, 208
Orwell, George, 156–7

Paine, Thomas, 205
Park, Katharine, 36
pathos, 133–5
perspective, 97–100, 104
Plato, 177
  Apology, 18–23
  Republic, 23, 24
  Symposium, 19–20
  Theaetetus, 15–18, 133, 135, 144
pride, 206, 220n2

reason
  in Burke, 59, 61–3
  in Descartes, 45
  in Kant, 66–71, 193–4, 198
  in Romanticism, 73–9
  in Spinoza, 40–2, 46, 216
refugees, 168–81
religion, 46–7, 52, 54, 86, 132, 183–7
revolution, 53, 180
rhetoric, 62, 156–7, 163, 174, 179
Romanticism, 41, 71–9, 80, 94–7, 99, 111, 187–90, 195, 197, 203n3, 215
Rousseau, Jean-Jacques, 64, 83, 180
Rubenstein, Mary-Jane, 208–9

Sand, George, 102, 105, 107
Sartre, Jean-Paul, 112–18, 155, 160–1
scepticism, 28–9, 108, 117–18
Schelling, Friedrich, 74–5
Schopenhauer, Arthur, 76–9
secular, the, 183–7, 201–2
Shelley, Mary, 79–87
Shelley, Percy Bysshe, 79
singularity
  in Derrida, 140–9
  in Heidegger, 129
  in Spinoza, 41–4
Smith, Adam, 49–50
sovereignty, 143–5
Spinoza, Benedict de, 30–2, 123, 129, 136, 141–3, 149, 164
  on imagination, 46–9, 157–8
  on pride, 206

on reason, 215–18
and Romanticism, 73–6, 189–90
on wonder, 36–50
stupidity, 93–4, 100–6, 113–18, 149–53, 175–6, 218–20
sublime, the, 126, 187, 188, 191, 198–203, 205, 213, 215
  in Burke, 52–63
  in *Fear and Trembling,* 88–90
  in *Frankenstein,* 80–2, 84–5
  in Kant, 68–71, 191–7, 198–9
  in Romanticism, 75, 76–9, 87, 94, 100
surprise, 31, 40, 49–50, 129, 133, 211; *see also* astonishment
sympathy, 58, 62

Tacitus, 179
taste, 54, 58; *see also* judgement: aesthetic
Taylor, Charles, 158–9, 184
Taylor, Jacqueline A., 220n2
time, 124–5, 145–8
tragedy, 54, 63, 77
transcendence, 183–90, 193, 197, 201, 203; *see also* religion
truth, 94, 96, 108, 127; *see also* objectivity

Voltaire, 92

war, 198–201
  'on terror', 162–3
will, 35, 39–40, 43–4, 45, 76–8
Wittgenstein, Ludwig, 132
Wollstonecraft, Mary, 79

EU representative:
Easy Access System Europe
Mustamäe tee 50, 10621 Tallinn, Estonia
Gpsr.requests@easproject.com

www.ingramcontent.com/pod-product-compliance
Lightning Source LLC
Chambersburg PA
CBHW051115230426
43667CB00014B/2595